MASS
MATTERS

REFLECTIONS OF A
PARISH PRIEST

WILLIAM J. BAUSCH

clear *faith*
PUBLISHING

Published by Clear Faith Publishing, LLC
100 Stevens Landing Dr., #206
Marco Island, FL 34145
www.clearfaithpublishing.com

Cover and Interior Design by Doug Cordes

The interior is typeset in Blacker and Molde SemiCondensed

ISBN: 978-1-940414-26-3

The mission of Clear Faith Publishing is to spread joy, peace, and comfort through great writing about spirituality, religion, and faith that touches the reader and serves those who live on the margins. Portions of the proceeds from our Homilists for the Homeless series are donated to organizations that feed, shelter, and provide counsel for those in need. For more information please visit us at www.clearfaithpublishing.com

DEDICATION

To my nephew, John Anderson,
who both in need and in deed,
is always there.

CONTENTS

INTRODUCTION: ABOUT THIS BOOK

The title *Mass Matters* is a play on words. The second word, in the upper case, is used as a verb and emphasizes that this ancient rite of Christian worship is central to our identity as Catholic Christians. However, when this word is in the lower case and used as a noun, it describes the parts that make up the Mass. This book is about both meanings. After examining a bit of the history of the Mass and the place of the parish church in our lives, I get into the inner furniture of the soul as it were, meaning the emotional attitudes we have in getting to church the public statement made by going to church, and, finally, the place of proper humility, silence, and reverence. After that, I take on cantankerously hypnotic smart phones, compulsive late-comers and those who leave-early, dysfunctional sound systems, weak lectors, grandstanding music ministers, over-pious celebrants, fussy deacons, misplaced church announcements, bad homilies, foreign priests, the new Hispanics, the overrated three-year lectionary cycle, the underrated parish bulletin, and widespread parish hopping. There are lot of good pastoral suggestions to remedy these defects and not a little crankiness to challenge your charity.

After exhausting these topics (and the reader) and liberally tossing around vital statistics, I invite the reader to probe deeper by focusing on the current radical and challenging issues that militate against churchgoing: empty seminaries (we're running out of priests), empty pews (we're running out of churchgoers), and empty replacements (we're running out of young people). I end with a proposal of a new alliance.

So, in one way this is a book about the liturgy, but it will soon become apparent that its consistent subtext, its real and deeper pastoral intent, is to offer the remnant—the people who loyally stay—a challenge to double-check unmet hopes and the dullness of routine and to reset their churchgoing lives in terms of making a statement, no matter what the experience or how they feel. It's a book meant to invite such faithful people to become more intentional Catholics, thereby seeding the future.

After each chapter, there are discussion questions to consider, plus some random pastoral suggestions (taken from my book *The Total Parish Manual*) that do not necessarily relate to the chapter but are offered as something that promotes parish community.

Who is the intended audience of this book? The general answer is anyone who is curious and interested in remaining a Catholic or who wants a fresh look at what attending Mass should be, could be, like. The specific answer is activists and ministry people who, in cooperation with their pastors, want to make the parish better and more appealing in these days of declining numbers and the stained atmosphere of the clergy sex scandals. Ideally, a parish interested in refreshing and recalculating its appeal and effectiveness might run discussion groups using this book as a focal point and template for discussion.

I leave you with the words of a noted convert and churchgoer, Blessed Dorothy Day:

> "The greatest challenge of the day is how to bring about a revolution of the heart, a revolution which has to start with each one of us."

ACKNOWLEDGEMENTS

I wish to express my gratitude to Jennifer Schlameuss-Perry, who cast an eye over the manuscript and aided me with compiling the websites and blogs, both foreign territories to me; to Deacon Vincent Rinaldi, Ray and Ellen Rugarber, Howie and Peg DePol, and Jack and Jane Davis for their encouragement and suggestions. I am particularly grateful to Lucille Castro, a long-time parishioner and friend, who gave so many hours trolling her considerable background to come up with persistently helpful corrections and wise suggestions. I am especially grateful to Christopher Bellito for his sharp editing, encouragement, and guidance.

PART I

TIME AND PLACE

This part examines the way we worshipped in the past, the centrality of the parish, the parish as local church and the gifts of religion.

1

THE MASS THEN
AND NOW

THESE PAGES SET UP the scene and provide a necessary overview of and context for what makes the Mass Matter. What
we call so casually "going to church" or "going to Mass" is a long
venerable practice. It's an ancient thing we do. We can trace it to
an upper room in Jerusalem about the year 33 of our era. We know
the celebrant and the first congregation. We know its basic outlines,
no matter how much it has been modified over the centuries: gathering, song, blessing, praise of Yahweh, bread broken, wine passed,
and the words, "take and eat and drink" in remembrance; that is,
break your life and pour out your deeds as I have done, and "I am
with you all days."

This scripture-blessing-taking and breaking and Holy Presence
have been and still are celebrated in hidden places, private homes,
dark prisons, underground, and in grand cathedrals. Yes, the Mass
is very old and, yes, it is being celebrated openly or clandestinely
somewhere around the globe as you read this. It is helpful every once
in a while to realize that we belong to a vast community of saints-
or as St. Paul uses the term, past, present, and yet to come. What
we take so casually has been and still is celebrated with joyous fear
and fearful joy.

But, to our point, the Mass has changed and the next time you go to church you are going to celebrate the latest version of it. And I don't mean just the relatively recent changes you are aware of, like the new translation of the Mass prayers, but those over the long haul from way back to its beginnings. Obviously, even in our own lifetimes, Mass wasn't always the way we know it. Some of you may recall the Latin Mass.

So, let's take a moment to hop, skip, and jump over the centuries.

The scene is a Passover-like devotional meal (although John will make it the actual Passover meal). Matthew 26:28 describes what happened. "While they were eating, Jesus took some bread, and after blessing it, he broke it, gave it to his disciples and said to them, 'This is my body'. Then he took a cup and, giving thanks, he gave it to his disciples saying, 'Drink from it, all of you, for this is my blood of the new covenant which is poured for many for the forgiveness of sin.'"

Luke (22:20) gives a slightly different version: "Then Jesus took a loaf of bread and, when he had given thanks, he broke it and gave it to his disciples saying, 'This is my body, which is given for you. Do this in remembrance of me.' Later he did the same thing with the cup after supper saying, 'This cup that is poured out for you is the new covenant of my blood.'"

Luke's "Do this in remembrance of me" started the whole thing off. And it continued as Jesus's disciples and first followers after his death took him literally. Right away after those Last Supper days, the first Jesus-followers ate together- whether in the humble hovels of the poor or, more often, the better homes of the more affluent who had more space. They remembered Jesus with bread, wine, hymns, and stories. In doing so, they experienced his presence, his friendship, and were reminded over and over again to "do this in his memory." Not to *believe* this but to *do* this; that is, do what we would come to call the spiritual and corporal works of mercy—bless, break, and share. Luke's Acts of the Apostles (2:46) records, "They devoted themselves to the apostles' teaching and fellowship and the breaking of the bread together…all who believed were together and had all things in common; they would sell their possessions and goods and distribute the proceeds to all…day by day, as they spent much time together in the temple, they broke bread at home…."

Of course, being human like us, they had their dissonant moments. St. Paul, writing in around the mid 50's, just some twenty years after Jesus' death, had to remind the people of Corinth to forget divisions—for example, who was high- or low-born and who were the Jews and who were the late-comer gentiles, or who was eating separately when they came to the Lord's Supper. Rather, "when you gather to eat, you should all eat together" (1 Cor. 11:33). Gradually at these supper meetings, hymns were sung, scripture were read, and instructions given. In short, we have the first Masses spoken in the vernacular of common Greek and celebrated in homes since early Christianity was illegal. The gathering was probably led by the home's host. We're not sure if the host was male or female. The prayers centered on thanksgiving (Eucharist) and were extemporaneous, although early on some became fixed into what we would later call the canons of the Mass. Communion was under both species. But, all the while, the "bread broken" kept its emphasis: just as Jesus broke himself for us, so must we do likewise for others. This, for the first 300 years of persecution, was what we might call the era of the Simple and Flexible Mass.

Things Get More Elaborate

Then around the 5th and 6th centuries we get the Long and Complicated Mass. What had happened, of course, was that the emperors Constantine and later Theodosius made Christianity the religion of the state. The upside to this liberation was felt by all those bishops and ordinary Christians who, finally free of persecution, could now worship openly as they pleased. The downside was that the Church, given official status by the Roman Empire, took on its structures, and soon imperial pomp soon invaded the sanctuary. Prayers grew more stylized and fixed. Solemn chants replaced familiar hymns and vested clergy led the worship. No longer were the people around the table. They were relegated to standing in the gathering space while only the clergy could preside at the altar. By this time, Christians were in cathedrals. By the Middle Ages, many laypeople received the "take and eat" Communion only once a year, and later not at all, so that the Church had to mandate that they receive at least once a year—the old "Easter Duty."

In short, everything is longer, grander, and more solemn. There are added prayers for the living and the dead, ceremonies borrowed outright from the Byzantine court ceremonials, including what early Christianity rejected as heathen practices such as genuflections, bowing, kissing, incense, and candles. The cults of the saints and martyrs flourished. It's a clergy-dominated, complex, and stratified worship.

The result was that, by the time of the 9th and 10th centuries, we get the Far Away and Silent Mass. For the first time in about a thousand years, there is silence. The reason that no one is talking or singing in church is because no one really understands Latin anymore. The choir has taken over all the singing parts and is now separated from the sanctuary and stuck over the entrance of the church. The sanctuary of the church has been decorated with a backdrop wall of sacred art and statues directly behind the altar that has been moved against it, thus forcing the priest to stand with his back to the people. The people's speaking parts have been taken over by altar boys. The people standing from midway to the back of the church could not see or hear. They at least wanted to see the Host and Chalice when they were consecrated so the Church had to introduce the elevation of the Sacred Species. Remember, the cathedrals were vast, and there were no electric lights or public-address system. We can appreciate the physical and emotional distance between the people and their Mass.

The fourth and final category, which persisted until Vatican II's revisions, was the Mass of the Rubrics. The 16th century Council of Trent, in a praiseworthy attempt to regulate the many abuses that had grown up around the Mass, put out strict rules and very minute directions or rubrics concerning everything from the way the priest wore the maniple (anyone know what that is?) to what to do if he dropped the Host. Trent inadvertently froze the Mass into a precise ritual passively watched by the people who said their private devotions in the pews. The public Mass of the clergy became a backdrop for the private piety of the laity.

The old Church had its faults and seeds of decline, of course. It could become insular and proud. Laws could be onerous. Clericalism was entrenched. Religious and ethnic prejudices sometimes showed their ugly sides. Sometimes the church appointments and decorations were over the top. At times they could be inappropriate and distracting from the primacy of the altar. Private devotions and rosary-saying during Mass were common enough. Lighting candles was more important than Communion while the people, passive and silent, attended "Father's Mass."

Vatican II Reforms: Pros and Cons

In the mid-sixties, the reforms of Vatican II were meant to correct this unbalance. As far as the liturgy goes, these reforms gave us the gifts of the vernacular, some marvelous hymns (after a slow start), participation by lay ministers and the congregation, and offered a more open church. Unfortunately, there was a downside. The liturgy reformers were limited to the university intellectuals who believed that, once the liturgy was understood and the people engaged in "active participation," they would no longer need the embarrassing distractions of baroque devotions. They were surely right up to a point. Again, some of those "non-liturgical" devotions *were* only tenuously tied to biblical realities; others were lurid, and some came close to outright magic. There certainly was need for reform and we're grateful for it, but, in some cases, it went too far.

We built churches that were functional, some were even close to being computer-like buildings, but we lost the sense of the beautiful—a rich source of awe and intimations of God's closeness. The focus was unerringly on the altar, and so any "clutter" had to be removed. The angels and saints disappeared. Clear widows replaced stained glass. Banners and representational art appeared. Gregorian chant was out. Novenas and parish missions were no longer around. Processions dried up. In a word, popular devotions, intractably connected to ethnic groups, went into a decline. This was so much so that nearly forty years after Vatican II the alarmed United States Conference of Bishops felt compelled to issue a strong statement defending popular devotional practices. The American bishops, as well as Popes John Paul II and Benedict XVI, encouraged the return of popular devotions. I might add this was just in time because, as we shall see, with the Pentecostal-leaning Latinos dominating the

American church now and in the future, there is a need to restore sensible devotions into the way we worship.

The New Translation

One priority of liturgical renewal was the translation of the Mass into the vernacular. The architects of the new Mass translation of 1998 left us a fairly reasonable and engaging product. However, the bishops decided to review the renewal and in 2011 they revised the Mass' translation. It has been a failure because they essentially bequeathed us a decidedly disenchanted and uninspired translation. The consensus is that it is, in the words of the highly regarded scholar Eamon Duffy, "a disastrously misconceived project." He continues, It is "archaic, verbose, and, in places, frankly unintelligible…larded with Latinate technical terms…The result is protracted sentences with multiple subordinate clauses, hard for priests to proclaim (Amen to that!) and for congregations to follow." Sometimes the priest and people shake their heads and ask, "What did I just pray?"[1]

It didn't have to be this way. We had a much better translation in the 1998 version, but the bishops were bulldozed into submission to accept the new version. The result is that today there is a real divide between those American Catholics who prefer the new vernacular liturgy of the Mass and the proponents of the pre-Vatican II Latin liturgy, a divide much wider and acrimonious in the United States than in other countries (some of them outright rejected the new translation). It's safe to say, I think, that the breach between conservative and liberal Catholics on other matters won't be solved until there's some kind of liturgical reconciliation.

All this history is not to say that, along the way and despite serious limitations, many beautiful additions have not enhanced the Mass. There were glorious oratorios, reflective Gregorian chants, magnificent Holy Week liturgies, and a deep sense of mystery which even the most dedicated champions of the modern revised vernacular Mass admit has been lost. I've always maintained this was because the officials in charge left the revisions solely in the hands of the heady professionals and failed to include the three essential P's—the pastors, the poets, and the people—in their search for a more relevant liturgy.

I suspect there are more changes to come, but still there remains that basic action of bread broken and shared—by Jesus, by us. There are the scriptures, the altar table, the hymns, and the people. They go way back. As a writer in *The New Yorker* magazine wrote, he was haunted by the thought of "the ancientness of the Mass—that it and its antecedents very likely go further back into the human past than any other existing ceremony…I began to feel that the Mass gave me a living connection with my ancestors…." We should try to get those feelings, not only of connection to the past but also of connection with the present, especially with our persecuted brethren who, as you read this, are breaking bread at their peril.

Yes, through all the changes over the centuries, these unchanging realities bring to memory the assurance that "where two or three are gathered together in my name, there am I in the midst of them"—especially in the Eucharist.

Discussion Questions

1. What do you think of the revised Mass?
2. How would you rate the liturgy in your parish?
3. Do you get anything out of attending Mass? If not, why not?

Pastoral Suggestion

For most parishes, people who want to join (and get their kids into CCD) simply drop into the parish office, sign up and, like the Lone Ranger, depart. We came at it differently. People picked up a form telling them they would be contacted. When we had enough people, we then invited them to an orientation ceremony to explain the purpose of the parish and arranged for various people to speak about our ministries. Then we gave them (1) a piece of a jigsaw puzzle, which at the end they all contributed to the overall photograph of the parish church. They also received (2) a plant to remind them that we will grow together, and we (3) asked them to bring a photo of themselves and their family (we took the photos if they didn't have any). The photos went into our parish files so we could identify them. They also appeared in the parish bulletin and on the church bulletin board so that others could welcome them. Then, of course, there were refreshments. By and large, the people were pleased. It gave a human face to the parish welcome.

2

THE IMPORTANCE AND IMPACT OF THE PARISH CHURCH

AN OBVIOUS TRUTH: FOR most people, Mass is celebrated in the communal space we call the parish church. We need to reexamine this basic unit of the Church that we take for granted. A gospel scene will set the stage.

Two disciples were staring at Jesus as he walked by. Jesus saw them out of the corner of his eye, turned and then said to them, "What are you looking for?" They said, "Teacher, where are you staying?" He replied, "Come and see." The two disciples went, and they saw. They saw Jesus seeking out the company of the excluded, the wretched, the sick, and the poor. They saw mercy, compassion, forgiveness, and new life. And, so, they came to believe. (John 1: 36-39).

Ponder slowly the truths this episode reveals. The underlying attraction of a parish is that people are looking for roots long before they are looking for beliefs. People are seeking the lived story long before its official formulations. People are forming relationships long before they embrace religion. In short, community comes before religion, belonging comes before believing, story comes before liturgy, and action comes before assent. The proper tactic of religion, therefore, is not to push dogma but to offer shared experiences. No one can be argued into faith. To fool people into thinking that they cannot enter a faith unless they first wholeheartedly believe is getting things backwards. In all the great religious traditions the prophets and mystics spent little time telling people what to believe. Rather, people were first invited to trust that, despite all the tragic things to the contrary, our lives do have some ultimate meaning and value. Faith, therefore, is the fruit of discovery, not something you must have at the beginning of the quest. Yes, community first and belief second must be the parish's strategy. "Come and see."

The Centrality of the Parish

For a long time, the parish Church in America had always been one of "come-and-see" attraction. It was one of the bedrocks of the faith and our link to the larger Church. It is the place where people, summoned out of their individualism to communal worship, most visibly become the Church. Parishes, like our schools, were built with great sacrifice and pride. When there used to be neighbor-hoods in America, the parish church was usually the "anchor store." It dominated the spiritual and social landscape. It supported and gave identity to the immigrants and, through its sacramental system, comforted people at every stage of life. In many places, like Phila-delphia and Brooklyn, neighborhoods were often identified by the name of the parish church.

The parish *was* important. As I once wrote, "...the average Catholic (including future bishops) gets his or her first and lasting impression of 'the Church' from the parish; it is there that the first incorporation into the Body of Christ takes place; it is there that the daily dramas of life, union, death, and resurrection are celebrated; and it is there that struggles, failures, and reconciliations occur. In short, the parish is the vital and critical hand that first rocks the ecclesiastical cradle, and so it's importance can hardly be overes-timated. For Catholics and non-Catholics alike, the parish forms a lasting impression of what the 'the Church' is all about."[2]

Yes, the old neighborhood parish, however insular at times, did provide the stories and symbols, sights and sounds of a religion that invited. Savor the following:

"The Catholic Church of yesterday had a texture to it, a feel: the smudge of ashes on your forehead on Ash Wednesday, the cool candle against your throat on St. Blaise's day, the wafer-like sensation on your tongue at Communion. It had a look: the oddly elegant sight of the silky vestments on the back of the priest as he went about his mysterious rites facing the sanctuary wall in the parish church; the monstrance with its solar radial brilliance surrounding the stark white host of the tabernacle; the indelible impression of the blue-and-white Virgin and the shocking red image of the Sacred Heart. It even had a smell, an odor: the pungent incense, the extinguished candles with their beeswax aroma floating ceilingward and filling your nostrils, and the smell of olive oil and sacramental balm. It had the taste of fish on Fridays and unleavened bread and hot cross buns. It had the sound of unearthly Gregorian chant and the mournful song, *Dies Irae*. The church had a way of capturing all your senses, keeping your senses enthralled."[3]

These powerful symbols, the iconography, the statues of the saints, the Latin, the stained glass windows, the Ember days, the Lenten fasts, the novenas, parish missions, and monthly confessions gave many a sense of *feeling* Catholic—especially if you lived in a kind of Catholic ghetto, and especially if the neighborhood in many subtle ways reinforced your Catholicism. There was a perceptible whiff of enchantment. The effect was the comfort of knowing who you were, of knowing that, with all those angels and saints, you were never alone.

No more. Like others, Catholics in the United States after World War II moved out of the safe ethnic monolithic neighborhoods of their immigrant forbearers to the suburbs. That transition encouraged an increasingly pluralistic and secular society where the private car and the cornucopian mall ruled. Suburban identities faded into the general mix. Anonymous big city living was not friendly to a communal religion like Catholicism. The bonds of the sustaining and reinforcing structures of family, neighborhood, and ethnic identity slowly became undone. They were undermined by private consumerism and a pervasive secularism. Individualism replaced community. The media replaced art. Celebrities replaced saints. "Rational" science replaced "irrational" belief. Wired, digital symbols replaced the vocabulary of the transcendent. There were benefits and there were losses in all this upheaval. The challenge to the modern parish, as we noted at the beginning of this chapter, is to focus on a sense of community, to offer a "come and see" other way of life.

Two Truths to Ponder

Meanwhile, when we do go to Mass, it is helpful to carry two truths with us.

The first is this: early on in Christianity, St. Paul began writing to some small, newly formed Christian communities scattered around the Mediterranean. His introductions grab us: "Paul, Silvanus and Timothy to the church of the Thessalonians," or "to the church of God which is in Corinth." Notice Paul said "to the church." Yes, the full Church of Jesus was in Thessalonica and Corinth. These churches were in no way subdivisions of the Church in Jerusalem. They were full independent churches united with the others by a common faith, baptism, Eucharist, and apostolic preaching. They were not subsidiary branches of the mother Church in Jerusalem. They were fully Church in themselves.

I point this out because, I suspect, our mental image of the Church is that of an industrial complex model with its clones all over the world. That is to say, the average Catholic, both clerical and lay, thinks of his or her parish as a subsidiary of the Vatican. The local parish is looked upon in relationship to the Vatican corporate headquarters in Rome as the local Chevrolet dealer is in relationship to General Motors at its the corporate headquarters in Michigan.

In fact, the only reason we have parishes, we think, is that the pope, who is the pastor of the universal Church, obviously can't handle the whole world, so he has CEO's called bishops who oversee the carved up smaller units called dioceses. But the bishop can't handle all his territory either, so he in turn subdivides it into parishes. The parish is the last subdivision, with the implication the parish exists only at the behest of the next higher level. It has no innate justification. It is but a branch office with all its standard "products" bought from the parent company. Most people subconsciously understand the local parish this way. It's what we call a vertical ecclesiology or vertical Church structure. The parish is a franchise under the brand name of Roman Catholic.

But this is clearly not so. You heard St. Paul. The local church exists in its own right and not just as an organizational, administrative sub-unit of the Church universal though connected to it. Vatican II's doctrine of collegiality was very clear about this. The bishops in their "Dogmatic Constitution on the Church" (26) remind us: "This Church of Christ is truly present in all legitimate local congregations of the faithful which, united with their pastors, are themselves called churches in the New Testament." Let me repeat this teaching: "This Church of Christ is truly present in all legitimate local congregations of the faithful which, united with their pastors, are themselves called churches in the New Testament." Let's continue:

> "For in their own locality these are the new people called by God, in the Holy Spirit and in much fullness. In them the faithful are gathered together by the preaching of the gospel of Christ, and the mystery of the Lord's Supper is celebrated…In these communities…Christ is present. By virtue of him, the one, holy, catholic and apostolic Church gathers together, for the partaking of the Body and Blood of Christ…."

Ramifications

I know this sounds somewhat esoteric, but it has ramifications. Think again: the full Church of Jesus is present in your local parish. The parish with its pastor, the bishop's representative, is not a mere subdivision of Rome or the diocese. It has its own integrity, shares a common mission, and is the full Church of Jesus Christ in union with others and the bishop of Rome (the pope) as symbol and capstone of that unity. Moreover, that Church—this church— is the People of God, to use the phrase of Vatican II, a people who have been called and commissioned by their baptism to be full, adult members presided over by a pastor who has been given Holy Orders; that is, his task is to bring a holy order to the gifts of the people which they possess, not by delegation, but by their own right as baptized members.

In other words, the pastor's task is not to share his or the bishop's power with the laity but rather to call forth and remind them of the power they already have in virtue of their baptism. The laity, in short, are collaborators—equal co-laborers—in the common task of the Church. Indeed, when you come right down to it, being 96% of the Church, the laity is its most public element.

Listen to the United States' Bishops: "One of the characteristics of lay men and women today is their growing sense of being adult members of the Church. Adulthood implies knowledge, experience and awareness, freedom and responsibility, and mutuality in relationships…thanks to the impetus of the Second Vatican Council, lay women and men feel themselves called to exercise the same mature interdependences and practical self-direction which characterizes them in other areas of life."

Pyramid to Circle

Those raised on the old paradigm of the Church may find all this challenging. They remember the pyramid church: there is the apex at which stands the pope, the "Vicar of Christ." At one more humble point in history, all he would dare claim was "Vicar of St. Peter." From there everything moves in a downward spiral to the cardinals, archbishops, bishops, monsignors, most reverend, very reverend, unbelievably reverend priests, deacons, religious, lay ecclesial ministers and, on the bottom, women. These clerical favored ones—remember, *they* had a vocation and were clearly marked as destined for heaven—have been called to the more perfect life (especially the celibate ones) and holiness trickled down from them. Notice, for example, that in the old calendar of the saints, eighty percent of them were clergy or religious. Burdened with worldly marriage, children, and a job, the remaining laity's humble hope was that at best they would slip into purgatory with a scorched rump.

This old pyramid is slowly moving to the circle as today the emphasis is not on the holy orders of the few but on the baptism of the many. Vatican II earnestly issued a *universal* call to holiness and reminded the laity of its witness to the world and to the Church itself. Take these sensibilities to church with you.

The Second Truth

Our second truth is a very modern concern: Going to Mass is actually good for you and you should know why. I bring the subject up because the secular culture, following Sigmund Freud, tends to treat anything religious as a neurosis requiring therapy. In fact, our secular society demands that religion should be banned altogether or at least excluded from the public square. In this it has been successful because religion, it maintains, is harmful to human potential. However, the truth is quite the contrary. A well-respected author, Gregg Easterbrook, writing in the *New Republic*, makes the case: "Recent studies indicate that men and women who practice in any of the mainstream faiths have above-average longevity, better immune system function, lower blood pressure, and fewer anxiety attacks, and they are far less likely to commit suicide than the population at large."[4]

The mention of suicide raises alarm bells. Very recent studies from the Centers for Disease Control and Prevention have reported that sadness and depression have increased from twenty to forty percent among adolescents, particularly teenage girls within the last twenty years. More ominously, it also reported in 2018 a twenty-five percent national increase in suicides. In 2016, for example, there were twice as many suicides as homicides. These studies have found that nearly 45,000 Americans aged ten or older had died by their own hand in 2016. All this is despite increased prevention efforts.

Social scientists are puzzled. They speculate about the usual causes: social isolation, lack of mental health treatment, drug and alcohol abuse, gun ownership, and so on. These reasons may be true, and we bless the people who press for reform. Still, constrained by official bias, the experts cannot bring themselves to make reference to the positive benefits of religion, certainly not as the whole answer, although a significant one.

The fact is that recent scientific research does emphasize that going to church weekly is good for you, and that regular religious attendance may add as much as two to three years to one's life. In 2014 a review of research into spirituality and mental health concluded, "Religion and spirituality have the ability to promote or damage mental health. This potential demands an increased awareness of religious matters by practitioners in the mental health field as well as ongoing attention in psychiatric research."

For us on the scene, there is no doubt that the support of regular worship at the parish- where people really look out for each other- helps tremendously to overcome social isolation. Church people do show up with dinner when friends are sick, visit them when they're down, and raise money for their operations. Probably a third of church members belong to some kind of small group, like Bible studies. Surveys do show that churchgoers have more contacts and social support than their un-churched counterparts. In short, there's a lot of one-on-one interaction, an awareness of what's going on, and we all know that social support is directly tied to better health.

Let's go back to Easterbrook, who goes on to cite the findings of a Dr. Harold Koenig of Duke University Medical Center who has calculated that, with regards to any mainstream faith, the association between religious participation and good health holds for almost all of Christianity and Judaism, and presumably for Islam, as well. "The main distinction," he says, "seems to be whether you are a regular practitioner." Also, on average, regular churchgoers drink less, smoke less, use fewer recreational drugs, and are less sexually promiscuous than others. In 2014 a review of research into spirituality and mental health concluded, "Religion and spirituality have the ability to promote or damage mental health. This potential demands an increased awareness of religious matters by practitioners in the mental health field as well as ongoing attention in psychiatric research." Another researcher observes, "I think there may be another factor. Any faith demands that you experience the world as more than just what is material and observable. They sense God behind so-called reality. They can experience a loving God in the ordinary and that is a mainstay of support."

We church-goers don't want to go around like some TV hucksters saying, "Come to church and live longer!" like we're selling a face cream that erases wrinkles. We just want to appreciate that, as naturally religious people, going to church supports better living.

We just want to appreciate the fact that going to church makes for physical, mental, and spiritual health.

Discussion Questions

1. The parish may still be the best venue for renewal. Agree or disagree?
2. What's your assessment of your parish?
3. Are you active in the parish? Why or why not?
4. Meditate on Pope Benedict XVI's words: "The only really effective apologia for Christianity comes down to two arguments, namely, the saints the Church has produced, and the art which has grown in her womb."

Pastoral suggestion

Parish hospitality is an elusive quality, but we know it when we see it. One can immediately sense its presence—or absence—as one enters church: the attractiveness of the building, the warmth of the people, the friendliness of the ushers, and the sense of camaraderie among the people. There are some things that help promote it. One is having greeters in the vestibule holding doors open or handing out the bulletins (if you do that sort of thing). A friendly pastor in evidence helps. So do things like good music, a parish bulletin board with photos of new members or a photo of the recently deceased. Perhaps a sign-in book for visitors (those who give a readable address will eventually receive an acknowledgment card via the ministry of our shut-ins). Parishioners are primed to approach and greet anyone seemingly new. A small booklet on the history of the parish in the vestibule adds to interest and welcome.

Then, to prime the pump for involvement, there's the "one-shot-piggy-back" personal letter from the pastor asking people who would not otherwise be involved to volunteer for one simple short-lived activity. The people need to know they're not being conscripted for a long haul sentence. The idea is that, experiencing this freedom, they might be open to more in depth commitments later on. Examples would be helping serving coffee and donuts on one Sunday, having different neighborhoods in the parish decorate the church for Christmas, or inviting twelve non-active people- six males and six females from ages from eight to eighty- to have their feet washed on Holy Thursday. It's the cumulative things that add up. It's the sense of ownership that promotes hospitality.

Finally, transparency and communication are vital to maintain hospitality and good will. In Surveys, people give high marks to their parishes for keeping them informed: the parish bulletin, websites, mail, and so on. Having a platform for dialogue, however, is another matter. It seems feasible, therefore, every once in a while, for parishes to send out surveys regarding the parish, the liturgy, Mass schedules, the leadership, and issues that may bother them.

PART II

THE ESSENTIALS

This part, the heart of the book, examines the way we go to church and what we bring to it.

3

BUYING INTO THE PACKAGE

WHEN I WAS LITTLE, even though times were tough way back then, my parents somehow would save enough money to take the family to the Jersey Shore for a week or two. Even then it was a challenge to get there with the packing and traffic and all the rest, but the memories we made are lovely. More than a half a century later, I managed to retire at the Jersey Shore- in Point Pleasant Beach, to be exact. Of course, much had changed, mainly the part about getting there. Today, visiting the Jersey Shore in the summer is like preparing for the Normandy invasion.

Besides getting stuff together, there is the endurance of getting to and through one of the most populous states in the country. There are, of course, fickle gas prices that yo-yo to the tune of the market. There are a zillion vehicles clogging the roadways. The turnpikes, parkways, and standard roads are backed up to Canada. The heat, the cowboy drivers, the traffic weavers, the breakdowns that exponentially back up traffic, the bumper-to-bumper pace—are all part of the routine hassle of getting there. And getting there is only the tip of the problem because, when you finally arrive, there's the question of parking in a town that has about 5,500 winter residents but hosts about a million in the summer. So, you spend about an hour riding around looking for a parking space, finally parking illegally, figuring that the fee for doing so is easier to endure than the outrageous parking fees or not finding a place at all. The whole venture requires planning, preparation, endurance, stamina, and a little cunning.

But you endure it because the payoff for a day at the beach is worth it.

And, besides, you soon learn that survival really comes down to a mentality, to buying into the whole package, as it were. You know the risk, the horrific traffic, the long confinement in the car, the wariness over those drivers out to get you, the possible hold ups, the parking challenge and so on. Still you set your mind and go. You even develop strategies over the years and, however well or ill the best-laid plans go, you know the trip is, as I said, part of the package and you accept it; you buy into it.

It's the same situation getting to stadiums for the game, visiting popular resorts, exploring the national parks, traveling abroad, visiting the grandkids 800 miles away, or standing in line for hours during the Black Friday sales, and so on. Annoyed or resigned, you buy into the whole enchilada because the ultimate goal is worth it. "It is what it is," as the saying goes. Live with it.

If only we would have the same mentality, the same philosophy, the same acceptance—yes, even the same resignation, if you will— when we go to church.

Getting yourself or the family together, trying to be on time, minding the traffic, finding a parking space, presuming a certain time frame (a 30-, 45-, or 60-minute venue), and slowly snaking out of the parking lot when it's over are all part of the package of church-going and we should accept this as a fact of life and make the most of it—and, hopefully, adopt a "it was worth it" attitude. After all, most commuters have come to terms with the crawling parkway or tunnel traffic. They leave home earlier, figure in possible delays, and, in general, have become philosophical about the whole process. Why not the same with going to church?

Mass a drag?

But for some, it doesn't seem to work out that way. For them, going to church is a duty, something to get out of the way before the "real" day begins. Deliberately or subconsciously, they arrive late. They leave early by taking part in the time-honored Catholic Cakewalk of down the center aisle, up to communion, back up the side aisle to escape to the car before Mass is over, hoping to avoid the crunch, especially if soccer or Walmart is calling them. Do people really want to be so stingy and calculating with God? No. I suspect it's just a habit, a frame of mind.

Realistically, we can hardly expect that people should feel the same way about a routine weekly event that evokes as much thrill as doing the weekly laundry. I mean, going to church on Sunday is not like visiting the Grand Canyon. Still, in going to church we need a certain subconscious spiritual sensibility that falls somewhere between a routine practice and a Bon Jovi concert.

A plan—well maybe not exactly a plan—but an embrace of "that's the way it is" is in order when we go to church, a certain mentality, as we seek to make the most of the experience. How can we make going to church a "worth it" part of our lives?

Again, the answer, as suggested, is that, like going to the beach or the concert, consider going to church as a package deal. In other words, once you make up your mind that this hour—or whatever time slot, the coming, the Mass, the going—belongs to the communal worship of God and the strengthening of the community—then you accept the plusses and minuses of coming and going, give it all you've got, and *give it the time it deserves*. That means arriving on time and, especially, not leaving early. Okay, snafus happen, but they should be the exception and not the rule as it seems to be for some.

Maybe the parish should delicately have a soft campaign to curb it. I say "delicately" because sometimes people *do* have to leave for a legitimate reason and we must respect that. Say a prayer for them and level no judgments or sour looks. But if leaving early is a habit just to beat the traffic or get to the early bird specials before the others, then that's not good enough. You wouldn't want guests who came to your dinner to bolt before coffee. Nor does the Lord want to see you bolt before the sacrificial meal is over. The final hymn is just that—final—not starting up the car in the lot while it's being sung in the church. Being stingy with God is not a good thing. You should not give the impression that going to church is something to get out of the way, or that you're getting a head start to get to that so-called "real" life out there. And, besides, do you really want to miss seeing or chatting a bit with your exiting parish family? The inconveniences we suffer waiting to exit to the parking lot fall into perspective in the light of the time with God's family.

Setting Priorities

So, let there be no suppressed sense of duty (no more acceptable than "Do I *have* to go to the shore?"), no come-late-leave-early dance ("Could you not spend one hour with me?") and, as we shall soon see, no carryon distractions, especially electronic ones. This is God-community-worship-witness time. Walmart can wait. Relax and enjoy. No hedging where God is concerned, as Wilbur Rees reminds us:

> I would like to buy three-dollars-worth of God, please.
> I would like to buy just a little of the Lord.
> Not enough to explode my soul or disturb my sleep,
> Not enough to take control of my life; I'll keep
> Just enough to equal a cup of warm milk,
> Just enough to ease some of the pain from my guilt.
>
> I would like to buy three-dollars-worth of God, please.
> I would like to find a love that's pocket-sized,
> Not enough to make me love a black man.
> Not enough to change my heart; I can only stand
> Just enough to take to church when I have time,
> Just enough to equal a snooze in the sunshine.
> I want ecstasy, not transformation.
> I want the warmth of the womb
> But not a new birth.
> I would like to purchase a pound of the eternal
> In a paper sack guaranteed or money back.
> You see, I would like to buy three-dollars-worth of God, please.

Discussion questions

1. What is your attitude on going to church? Anticipation? Duty? Dread?
2. Do you regularly come late or leave early? If regularly and not just now and then, what is this telling you?
3. How can you change the habit?
4. Could staying to the end start out as a Lenten project that you might continue?
5. Let's leave you with a smile:

    A couple is walking out of church one Sunday. The wife asked her husband, "Did you see the strange hat Mrs. O'Brien was wearing?"

    "No," said the husband.

    "And did you notice those poorly-dressed children in the pew ahead of us?"

    "No, I didn't," replied the husband.

    "Bill Smith badly needs a haircut, doesn't he?" commented the wife.

    "Sorry, but I didn't notice," was the husband's response.

    "You know, John," said the wife impatiently, "sometimes I wonder if you get anything out of going to church."

Pastoral Suggestion

In the spirit of the last chapter's suggestion, let me offer "The Cracker Barrel." It's a kind of now-and-then town hall meeting with the pastor. Very informal. Open to all. Snacks and drinks are in order. I sit on a raised platform and proclaim, "All right. What do you want to talk about? Here's your chance to ask questions you always wanted to ask but were afraid to." The questions often start off mildly, like "How come Frank Sinatra got Christian burial?" and then move to today's, "How come people can marry, divorce, remarry and still go to Communion?" These Cracker Barrel meetings are fun and satisfying. They give people a platform to express their questions about many churchy things. Highly recommended.

4

MAKING A STATEMENT

IN THIS CHAPTER, WE widen our scope as we are invited to consider three reasons why "going to church," as we say today, makes a statement. These reasons are very important and, when considered prayerfully, may give us a new attitude and a new motivation to anticipate the journey.

First, we begin by suggesting that, if we are resigned or indifferent in going to church, it's because our world is too small. It's all about *I* am going to church, *my* effort, *my* car, *my* traffic, *my* envelope, or *my* piety. For those who measure life by their own feelings, the attitude is that "they should be glad I'm there at all," as though they were invited to a party and are doing the host a favor by showing up. For them, it's a personal, optional choice. The old defining Catholic truisms of the Mystical Body of Christ and the Communion of Saints have faded in an era of individualism and no longer have any bearing. The gospel parables of being urgently invited to the banquet have lost their force.

But going to church should not be a personal option. Going to church should be a communal imperative to answer God's living summons. We are not alone. Going to church is an affirmation of our "Catholic-ness," that we are one Body in Christ and that our "I" supports and is part of the "we." Going to church is a global affair. Our church-going, getting ready for church, and getting there and staying there is not a bit of personal piety. These are actions that put us in solidarity with countless others whom that very day will answer the same summons. As Richard Rohr puts it, the Eucharist is an invitation to socially experience the shared presence of God.

It's not an exaggeration to say that, in a very real sense, the Church comes into existence in these worldwide assemblies. Going to church is about giving over part of myself to all other believers with the conviction, as someone expressed it, that "my presence on Sunday is necessary for the Church's mission." Going to church underscores both our belief in the Communion of Saints and the value of community, of what it means to belong to the Catholic Church. As one writer put it:

> "Why sing a hymn with everyone else when I prefer the experience of singing alone? Why pray a psalm with the People of God when I get more out of praying in the privacy of my room? Because in Catholicism, joining together to pray, coming from all corners of our towns and villages, is an enactment of what it means to belong to the Catholic Church, to begin with. To pray together, to worship together, this is what it means to belong to the Church.
>
> …Going to Mass is not fundamentally about my unique spiritual experience, but about giving over part of myself in love to all other believers so that together we can manifest Christ's love for the world. Even if I'm distracted by work, dealing with a sick toddler, or more interested in watching a football game later in the afternoon, my presence on Sunday is necessary for the Church's mission of divine love. The Church is 'Catholic' because her destiny is to gather the human family into the peace of Christ's love." [5]

This notion of response to God's call, this sense of unity, is our statement that we are truly "Catholic" when we go to church.

The Competitions

The second way that going to church makes a statement is kicked off by this question: *What happens when Walmart moves into the neighborhood?* Answer: Within a 20-mile radius, all of the small Mom and Pop stores and the neighborhood services will disappear. They are absorbed by the box stores that can underprice them until they go broke. The gain is lots of stuff bought cheaply from anonymous strangers at one humongous site to which you bring your car and search for a parking place. The loss is community. The loss is interacting with people you know and trust, and neighborhoods where you could walk. So, Mom and Pop get in the car and now work for the Big Store while their children are looking like everybody else.

The post-World War II GI Bill allowed Catholics, for the first time, to enter secular colleges and move into the professional mainstream; as the glue of the neighborhood became unstuck, everyone escaped to suburbia. In the melting pot of suburbia, Catholic identity began to unravel. The grandchildren of the European immigrants were homogenized into secular "Americans" who no longer spoke the language, kept the customs, or went to church. Corporate capitalism, education, upward mobility, and, in our time, the total ubiquity and flattening process of the media, the internet, communication via the gadget, and the triumph of secularism have produced a population of identical brand name consumers.

The long-term result is that Catholics are now indistinguishable from their fellow citizens in terms of ethical values, social mores, and cultural tastes. They divorce, abort, practice contraception, vote, and consume like everyone else. Many, especially the educated, are too embarrassed to have a crucifix in their bedrooms or holy water fonts in the children's rooms, wear religious medals, eat fish on Friday or hot cross buns for Lent, or even go to Church. They no longer make a statement different from all others.

Well, I may have overdone this description to some degree, but there is no doubt that, in general, Catholics are no longer an identifiable cohort; they now live in a thoroughly secular environment. Therefore, it is important that you understand when you do "keep the Sabbath" you are making a countercultural statement. It is an old strategy and an old defiance.

The Sabbath or Sunday concept as 'making a stand' goes back to our Hebrew forebears. As resident slaves when they were in captivity in Babylon, they were daily corralled into the wretched routines and indignities as less than human moving parts of an oppressive society. Finally, they rebelled. In accordance with their covenant, they wanted, they declared, one day without work to worship their God. Their captors scoffed and doubled their chores and punishments, but the Hebrews persisted. They held a sit-down strike and would not move. Ultimately, the Babylonians, realizing that no working slaves meant economic collapse, gave in and let them have their Sabbath. When asked why they needed one day of rest, the Hebrews answered, "To remind ourselves that we are more than workers."

Jews, Muslims, and Christians have variously adopted Friday, Saturday, and Sunday as a time of worship, relaxation, contemplation, and for the enjoyment of Creation's wonders. Even in writing this, the dissonance of this scenario with present day reality is powerfully apparent when our Festival Days are dedicated mainly to shopping, soccer, and speed! Pope Francis has warned us about "rapidification," where speed exceeds our ability to comprehend and humanize the course of human events.

More Than

In today's jargon, our forebears were making a statement: "We are more than workers." *Yes, we are more than.* How desperately we need to embrace that truth! That phrase should be the first thing we say when we wake up. It should be enshrined in our hearts and placed over the entrance of every church. *We are more than.* That's why we're here in church: to affirm this truth.

In today's society, that means a great deal; furthermore, if you will, it's our contribution to evangelization. Although going to church may be routine, you should consider that you are making that defining statement: "I do not live by bread alone, even if my lifestyle sometimes betrays me." All day long we are identified and evaluated by where we live, what we do, how we dress, look, smell, perform, and produce. Going to church is our statement that shouts, "We are more than these things." In short, going to church is a statement that "it's not all about me, but about us and who we are."

Do we think of any of these things when we come to church? Hardly! We're worried about the pot roast in the oven or who has Mass today. Still, it's an awareness that, now and then, needs to be raised. We are here because we are "more than." Maybe going to church is the only time and place where we can state this truth so publicly.

Thinking Globally

Finally, may I add this unique imperative?

Yes, every Sunday the Catholic (universal) Church all over the world gathers her children to the Eucharist. The people of the continents, the islands, and earth's four corners respond. The high and mighty, the lowly and powerless, the rich and poor, the inhabitants of the cities and slums, the well and the sick, the unbelievers and the searchers, the peaceful and the troubled, and the free and the persecuted *all* answer the call. Here we pause to consider that we need to remember this last category. The people in Yemen, Egypt, Nigeria, Syria, and other places go to church with deep apprehension and terrible fears of murderous attacks on their minds because it's happened so often before. They have lost family, friends, and clergy. There are too many routine headlines like, "ISIS claims responsibility for the killing of 45 (33, 78, and the numbers get higher and higher) at this or that Christian church."

These people worship, if possible, in a church, but for some the worship takes place in secretly designated homes, farmhouses, hidden cellars, or camouflaged hideouts. Those in the prisons of the world await one special fellow prisoner who has managed to scrounge a piece of bread and a bit of wine and then sneaks it into the squalor of their cells where he celebrates Mass with them. All over the globe on any given Sunday millions of us, we the Church of every incarnation, answer that summons to renew the face of the earth. It would behoove us in our ordinary casual routine of getting to Mass on time to remember our brothers and sisters worldwide for whom it costs so much. Going to church is a statement that also says we are in solidarity with the persecuted Church.

Church is "boring." It is, so it is too many times. "Boring" is the word. But so is getting dressed, making the coffee, doing the laundry, the daily grinding commute every single day to work or school and changing the sheets every week, but it is these stable dependable routines and rituals which anchor our lives and keep them from chaos. They are the taken-for-granted boundaries that keep us safe. It's only when you can't dress yourself or make your own coffee anymore that you realize how much you miss the boredom.

Discussion Questions

Ponder this: Here's a dozen reasons someone collected about why people stay away from church:

1. I stay away from church because it rains. *You go to work in the rain.*
2. I stay away from church because it's hot. *So is the golf course.*
3. I stay away from church because it's cold. *It's warm and friendly inside.*
4. I stay away from church because I am poor. *There is no admission charge.*
5. I stay away from church because I am rich. *We'll take care of that.*
6. I stay away from church because no one invited me. *People go to the movies without being asked.*
7. I stay away from church because I have children. *God loves them.*
8. I stay away from church because there are hypocrites there. *You associate with them daily.*
9. I stay away from church because my clothes are not expensive. *It's not a fashion show.*
10. I stay away from church because the church always wants money. *So does the government.*
11. I stay away from church because I have company. *They will admire your loyalty, whether you bring them along or ask them to wait until you get back.*
12. I stay away from church because I have plenty of time to go later. *Are you sure?*

Another Truth to Ponder

There are times when we just don't feel like going to church just as we don't feel like going to school or work—but we do because examples matter. Researchers have shown that when students were given a test and were (1) graded by a teacher, and (2) had to sign an honor code, they cheated only somewhat. But when allowed to grade themselves, they cheated twice as much. Conclusion: moral reminders made the difference. Researchers have also found that role models, people who acted morally and sympathetically, inspired much more empathy and moral action from bystanders than those who had no role model. So, going to church is a reminder that you are an "other" making a deliberate act of role modeling. You are making a moral statement.

Pastoral suggestion

This suggestion, I grant, is unusual and not practical for everyone—in fact, it's far out—but, as the sole priest in the parish, almost every Saturday night I would invite anywhere from six to nine people in for dinner at the parish house (rectory). I asked people who I was fairly sure did not necessarily know each other. I would cook for them (if I had the Saturday evening Mass, I would resort to the crockpot strategy.) I would ask someone from our Singles' Group to act as host: welcome the people or offer drinks while I finished up in the kitchen. For twenty years the payoff was inestimable. I got to know people and vice versa—you can't eat and drink with them and fail not to. I got them to meet one another and learned something of their background. The novelty, community-building, and public relations impact were beyond measuring, not to mention that I truly experienced this as an extension of the Eucharist. Today, when so many priests have several parishes to minister to and lack the comfort and support of a single parish community, this may prove to be a necessary support. For the culinarily-challenged priest, have the folks bring dinner and just supply the hospitality.

5

A VESTIBULE REFLECTION

YOU'VE ARRIVED AT CHURCH. As you enter the main body of the church, is there a tension between fellowship and a sense of holy ground, or between chit chat and silence? Tricky issues.

Let me gently set up the problem by relating this strategy. Every five or six years during the after-the-summer month of September, when things come to life again, I would have sent out name tag stickers to all the parishioners asking them to magic-marker their names on them and wear them to church. (For those who forget, ushers were at the ready to supply them.) Before Mass began, I would ask the people to turn to one another and introduce themselves. This was always a pleasant and happy interchange and we would do it for the whole month. Other times we would move the sign of peace to the beginning of Mass. Conversation, greetings, and camaraderie are good ways to begin.

I have to tread lightly when I ask if all this ever eventually segues into awareness that we are on holy ground or, on the other hand, does there remain a kind of leftover marketplace atmosphere that we brought with us? Is there a sense of sanctuary? This feeling is indicated by the subtle shift from the vertical to the horizontal, that is, from a sense of something or "Someone" beyond us to only us, from the awesome Alpha and Omega to our interests. Or let me express it by observing that the felt sense of otherness, of mystery, seems to have evaporated. It's a loss that even the progressive liturgists mourn. The scriptural admonition," Remove the sandals from your feet, for the place on which you are standing is holy ground" (Exod. 3:5) has become a challenging command for an over-stimulated generation raised on an American sense of democracy where all lines have been erased. Reverence doesn't come easily.

In this brief chapter—more like a meditation—uneasily I muse about reverence and silence. Again, these are tricky issues. I surely don't want to dispense with the folksy camaraderie of familiar friends who meet weekly. As pastor, I liked to walk around the church to nod a welcome. Having greeters is a great way to welcome parishioners and visitors. The name-tag routine I mentioned is effective. Chatting after Mass, eating donuts, and sipping coffee in the parish hall afterwards is standard fellowship. A friendly community is the best advertisement for the faith. What I have in mind, however, is the *excessive* kind of "mall" chatter and "mall" overtone that I have encountered in some parishes. Yes, "mall" is the right metaphor.

The Buzz

I know that people addicted to around-the-clock noise tend to find silence of any sort quite intolerable. I know that business is a hallmark of importance in modern society. Perhaps, too, the emphasis on celebration and overly wordy liturgies has dulled our appetite of an "otherness" sense. Maybe there is little sense of reverence, either because the architecture is uninspiring (the church looks like Home Depot) or distractions are the order of the day. In any case, a mall atmosphere intrudes. At one parish I know, the folk group loudly practices before Mass. Ushers exchange small talk. In-the-pew conversations go on. Smart phones are checked. The sacristy is a little clubroom full of chatter. There's a distinct buzz. The flickering of the old sanctuary lamp conveys nothing anymore. A kind of background hum lingers.

I think of Dorothy Day. Even before she was converted she would sometimes attend Mass nearby and be enthralled. Of the experience she wrote that she "knelt in the back of the church, not knowing what was going on at the altar, but was warmed and comforted by the lights and the silence, the kneeling people and the atmosphere of worship. People have so great a need to reverence, to worship, to adore." Maybe they still do, but too often the reality is that anyone who comes to church early to catch a few moments of reflection and silence will have to look elsewhere. For some people church is a busy place, but not necessarily a prayerful place.

Contemplate this image: Before the beginning of a symphony, the conductor holds his baton erect to call forth silence. Then, after the silence is established, comes beautiful music. The silence is necessary to frame the beauty of the music. So it is with our spiritual lives. The great modern spiritual guide, Thomas Merton, wrote:

> "Let there always be quiet, dark churches in which men can take refuge. Places where they can kneel in silence. Houses of God filled with His silent presence. Here, even when they do not know how to pray, at least they can be still and breathe easily. Let there be a place somewhere in which you can breathe naturally, quietly, and not have to take your breathing in continuous short gasps. A place where your mind can be idle, forget its concerns, descend into silence and worship the Father in secret." [6]

Jesus often went apart by himself to think and pray. The Desert Fathers learned deep wisdom in solitude. The mystics proclaim again and again the value of silence. Modern psychiatry praises its value as a condition for mental health and for living a balanced life. Social workers catalog the moral and emotional wreckage of the overextended, overburdened life.

I admit that creating an atmosphere of worship, achieving the balance between the rituals of welcome and the mood of silence combined with a sense of both common and holy ground is a hard one to achieve, especially, I think, for a generation longing for the transcendent while burdened with an anemic sense of the hierarchy of things. I think I'm baying at the moon here, but all I wanted to convey is that we must find some way to be mindful of holy ground and holy silence when we, as Church, go to church.

Discussion Questions

What do you think of this: Rabbi Abraham Joshua Heschel wrote that we take a break from the distractions of the world, not as a rest to give us more strength to dive back in, but as the climax of living. By cutting off work and technology, we enter a different state of consciousness, a different dimension of time.

Pastoral Suggestion

Once a year, offer the Anointing of the Sick at a parish Mass. The difference? Invite the community's caregivers, the town's first aid squads, fire fighters, nurses, physicians—anyone in the health and emergency business—as a way of acknowledging their work within the community.

6

GOING TO CHURCH DISARMED

THE LONG WIND UP.

There it is, one of those clever *New Yorker* cartoons: two hip young executives—briefcases, beards, tattoos, Brooks Brothers suits—on a Wall Street pavement standing side by side yet facing opposite directions, each with their cellphone glued to an ear with one about to leave. The caption is, "Nice talking to you, Al."

The cartoon's zinger is that we can no longer communicate directly face to face with one another without a mediating phone or gadget. This emotional and personal distancing has reached epidemic proportions. Today many corporations charter outdoor camps which specialize in teaching their employees how to go through the withdrawal of living without 24/7 cell-phoning. Families and individuals are seeking help. The writer Andrew Sullivan wrote an article which got a lot of attention. It was entitled, "I Used to be a Human Being," and described what it's like to have your soul hollowed out by the web.

The stats: Today 98% of children from newborn to age eight access mobile devices at home compared with 52% in 2011. Ninety percent of Americans own a cellphone and many are addicted to their mobile devices. Think *you're* not addicted? You may be if, according to a Pew survey, you are among the sixty-seven percent who check your phone or messages when your phone doesn't ring or vibrate. One survey found that we check our phones 22 times a day—about every 4.3 minutes, and we use it 80 times a day or 30,000 times a year! The average person spends 11 hours a day looking at a screen of some kind.

There are other telltale signs. Are you anxious when you don't have your cell or smart phone, uncomfortable when you accidently leave it at home, restless till you get it, spend time on it when there might be better and more productive things to do? Do you feel the need to use it even when there's really no reason? Have you gotten what is called "text neck" pain from looking down at the phone or tablet too long?

The thing is, it's hard not to like our phones, those gadgets that provide so many useful functions. The awesome gifts of the Big Five—Apple, Amazon, Google, Microsoft, and Facebook—are so embedded in our lives, commerce, politics, entertainment, and military that literally we can't function or live without them. They belong to the "too big to fail" pantheon even if, as in the case of Facebook, the floodgates of false information, hacking, lies, hurtful rhetoric, and foreign interference have burst open. They also have a darker side, namely, that smart phones make us dumb and less social, and less open to the spiritual life. They affect our thoughts and judgments and, most of all, they are powerful, preeminent, progressive, and perennial distractions. Social media keeps pushing us on to the next distraction so that we are losing our ability to savor the moment. Our Catholic tradition has always urged us to be aware of the "sacrament of the present moment," to pause and reflect. The tradition of *lectio divina*, reading the scripture aloud and meditatively, is meant to achieve this. Instead we are cultivating a culture of distraction and are increasingly disconnected from the people and events around us.

Smart phones distract even when not in use. Studies show that, just being present, smart phones distract students and workers and affect their performances. Experiments illustrate that when our phones ring or buzz while we're in the midst of some challenging task or intensive need of attention, our focus wanders and work gets sloppier whether we answer the phone or not. *Again, just their presence distracts.* Studies also show that when people hear their cell phones yet are unable to answer them, blood pressures spike and problem-solving skills decline. Again, their mere presence diminishes our intelligence. For example, students who had their phones in view posted the worse scores in testing. Those, however, who left the phone in a different room did better. Those who kept their phones in their backpacks came out in the middle. Other studies showed that students who didn't bring their phones to the classrooms at all scored the best.

The Electronic Elephant in the Room

In a PBS documentary, one teacher says, "In a career that spans 38 years, I have not seen any single diversion that so distracts students from reading, writing, thinking, and working. When the cellphone is in front of them, they are completely focused on it. When the cellphone is in the backpack, they are worried because they can't see it. On the first day of class, I tell them that if they can't go 57 minutes without checking their cellphones, they have a problem and need to seek professional help. They laugh. I laugh, but I know how true that is. Only when I tell them to take their cellphones and put them inside their backpacks do they understand how accurate my diagnosis is." He agrees that for some classroom tasks the cellphone is helpful, but even here the students are off elsewhere. "Their bodies are in the classroom, but their minds are inside their cellphones," he says. Because this is so patently true, beginning with the 2018 school year, France has banned the use of smart phones from schools entirely with the rare exceptions for educational use and students with disabilities.

Not only do the smart phones dumb down our reasoning but they also retard our social skills and relationships. Smart phones, with their endless connections and apps, their speed and portability, are "supernormal stimuli" that hijack and consume our attention, and, as a side effect, because they are living encyclopedias, shut down our brains. I mean, why do the work when we can look it up? The smart phone, so filled with instant information, lowers the need to think as the mind outsources more and more to the gadget. Addiction, alienation, and distraction are powerful side effects from the benefits of amazing science.

The Pitch.

So, after that long wind up, now we come to the pitch. The conclusion is obvious: Our love affair with, and our addiction to our gadgets, is a spiritual issue. I, like everyone else, see people coming out of their cars and into the church vestibule fully engaged on their cellphones. Mass is barely over and their feet hardly out of the church proper when the cellphones are whipped out. Who knows, perhaps during those forty-five minutes the pope or the president called? What matter of worldwide import needs your attention? What if, while you were at Mass, Apple put out a new and wonderful smart phone and you missed the news? What *are* the Kardashians doing?

I haven't even mentioned the hardcore group who text *during* Mass. (I won't even mention the angst I feel when I see the celebrant, the deacon, or lector in the sacristy before Mass on the smart phone!) The Pope said, "At some point, the priest during Mass says, 'Lift up your hearts.' He does not say 'Lift up your cellphones....'" But some still do anyway. *The New York Times* had an article about people at St. Patrick's Cathedral in Manhattan[7] noting some worshippers accessing their smart phones. One woman even strode through the nave while Mass was going on wearing earbuds and chatting out loud all the while. One young woman with head bowed never looked up until she had ordered a pair of black boots off the internet on her iPhone. Later, when questioned, she replied with typical deadly American individualism, that she finds connection with God on *her own time, in her own way.* So much for communal worship!

At the beginning of Mass, cantors around the land announce something like this: "In deference to the sacred liturgy, please turn off all cellphones." But, some would argue, the habit is too ingrained, especially for people who were born with an iPhone in their hands, and the Church might as well create an app for use during Mass. Some few churches do precisely that. Still, nevertheless, despite any announcements, despite warnings, we are at the point when we feel emotionally naked without our phones. As we have seen, even if we do turn them off, *just having them with us* is a built-in distraction especially if it vibrates during Mass. To paraphrase the teacher cited above, "Our bodies are in church, but our minds are inside our cellphones."

Why then, outside of being addicted, would you bring your cell phone to church at all? Yes, it's hard not to, but it clearly, though subconsciously, signals to God that you have a distracted heart. Wouldn't you prefer that the doctor who is operating on you, the parent who is consoling a distraught child, or a partner making love would have left his or her cell phone somewhere else? Conclusion: to come to church with a divided heart—even though we don't think of it that way (but now you know)—compromises the mandate to love God "with your whole heart, soul, and mind."

Entering the sacred liturgy with a distracted mind and heart is not ideal, any more than entering the highway with a phone in your ear. Yes, come to Mass phoneless. Again, remember, even having them, as studies show, even if you do not use them, *is* a distraction. I know it is hard—it feels like coming to church without your shoes and socks on. It will take time. Still, I know some families who have courageously banned all cell phones from the dinner table. It can be done.

Therefore, I propose a three-step plan. First, leave your gadgets in your car. Give them a rest. Give yourselves over to sacred space and sacred worship with receptive minds and hearts. Better, as a parish, make it a crusade, a project, even a point of honor and, ultimately, a parish point of identity: "We're a parish who does not bring cell phones to church"—right up there with "We're a parish who stays till Mass has ended."

Second, for those who want a step up—and it *is* that—here it is: leave all cellphones and gadgets home altogether. Don't even leave them in the car. This way, after Mass you and the kids won't be racing to the car to grab the phone like an addict needing a fix— and I use that comparison deliberately. Withdrawal is hard! It would make a statement to the kids that there are priorities in life.

Third, for the deeply serious, look forward to giving up the cellphone for Lent or, as a good practical compromise, do it gradually and, say, give it up for the Fridays of Lent or maybe even another day of the week. It's a start, the beginning of regaining your soul. Best of

all, make it a communal parish Lenten project, as earnest and difficult as giving up chocolate. If you want to be clever, encouraging, and
find support, have a parish decal made for your car: "St. Gregory's
Parish: smoke free, gadget free." That will draw attention.

Bottom line: Giving full praise for the gadgets that let workers
gather knowledge, students conduct research, friends keep in touch,
and grandparents rejoice in grandkids a continent away, let's also be
mindful of the downsides and forge a new determination to make
our gadgets servants instead of masters. We can also let it be known
far and wide that, when it comes to going to church, what Jesus said
to Mary while Martha was on the cell phone—"She has chosen the
better part"—is our motto.

Discussion Questions

1. Recalling the "religion is good for you" theme in Chapter 2, ponder the following.
    Extensive evidence suggests that human relationships are in deep decline since
    social media has dominated and family life has collapsed. Most children born to
    mothers under thirty are born outside marriage. Suicide rates are at a thirty-year
    high. Depression rates have upped tenfold since 1960. Loneliness is now almost
    an epidemic. In the 1980s, twenty percent of Americans said they were often
    lonely. Now forty percent say so. In 2012, 5.9 percent of young people suffered
    from severe mental illness. By 2015, it was 8.2 percent. Teenagers spend more
    time alone with their digital screen; the greater the screen time, the greater
    the unhappiness. (In the current jargon, they are called "screenagers.") Eighth
    graders who are heavy users of social media are twenty-seven percent more likely
    to be depressed. Heavy internet users are much less likely to have contact with
    their neighbors. Physically, mentally, socially, and spiritually going to church gad-
    get-free has benefits in the sense that taming the gadgets there may hopefully
    spill over to domestic and social life. Need we add that if we spend eleven hours a
    day looking at a screen, there is less time to spend in meditation and prayer?

2. Reflect: Making Mass Matter should be a whole heart and mind project. How can
    you make it so?

3. Do we realize that turning off the gadgets or, better, as we said, not bringing them at all makes a statement about priorities?
4. Can you get your parish to start a "no gadgets" in church campaign?
5. A smile: after a short trip to Earth, the Martian astronaut arrives back and presents his superiors with a TV screen and a smart phone. "Sorry," he says, "that I couldn't capture and bring back any Earthlings, but I did better than that: I brought back two of their gods."

Pastoral Suggestion

Most parishes understandably have a few gifted people who decorate the parish church at Christmas. Usually it's the same dedicated people who do it each year and the result is lovely. We were willing to sacrifice some of the expertise by having parish neighborhoods do the task each year. There would be a neighborhood captain who would gather the folks, practicing or non-practicing, Catholic or non-Catholic, and they would come with drinks and sandwiches to decorate the church. There were guidelines that were augmented and passed on over the years. The results may not always have been shopping-window quality but was always nice. What I was after was ownership, community building, and, these days, perhaps, a chance for ethnic groups to incorporate some of their traditions.

7

THE ASSEMBLY OF THE BROKEN

IF BY GOING TO church we are making a statement, we should also be going as who we are, which is to say, beloved but broken. Both are essential attitudes to bring to church, but they seldom surface. Let me explain.

There are the people who treat going to church like visiting a country club: a pleasant place with such nice people who dress nice, and who greet and smile at one another.

At the same time, because we're human, we are also full of secret doubts, fears, yearnings, questions, pains, and sins of one sort or another. Yes, soon after we get there, we *do* acknowledge our limitations and confess to one another our faults *in a public setting*, although that startling thought, dulled by routine, never occurs to us especially if, after the celebrant invites us to confess our sins, in a millisecond he leads: "I confess to Almighty God, that I have greatly sinned in what I have done and failed to do...through my fault, through my most grievous fault...." So, with no time to pause for a quick examination of conscience, we tend to mumble through the confession mindlessly and move on. We stand. We sit. We smile and give the sign of peace. We're all "fine" when someone asks us as we stand beneath a cross on which hangs a beaten, nearly naked man suffering publicly on our behalf.[8]

The Downstairs Church

But something is missing, something in contrast to what occurs in many parish churches, not on Sundays but on weekday nights, and not *in* church but *under* it. Yes, it's usually in a church basement that the holiest hour of the week takes place because it's there where a mismatched group of CEOs, single moms, doctors, accountants, victims of clergy abuse, housewives, and homeless veterans share in the communion of strong coffee and dry pastries and engage in the sacred act of telling one another the truth.

They admit their powerlessness and dependency. They conduct inventories of themselves. They confess to God, to themselves, and to one another the exact nature of the wrongs. They ask for help. They summon up the courage to expose their darkness to light: "My name is Shelia and I'm an alcoholic." Yes, it's an AA meeting.

If we came to church with the AA mentality then Mass might be more meaningful, not just something to be endured. If we come with my favorite prayer on our lips—"O God of the Second Chance, here I am again!"—it would open us up to God's saving presence and the sense that here is where we should be. There are other attitudes to also embrace, such as we come to church not so much to seek answers as to find the strength to live the questions. We come not to seek certainties—only atheists claim certainty—but trust. We seek not solutions but hope. We come to church not only looking for a cure but, more deeply, for healing. One refers to the body, the other to the soul. We come to find the strength to enter into the broken lives of others and hold them in love. We come to church because we can't be Christians on our own, and because salvation is communal. We come because these words, written by a young adult, also belong to us:

> "Now, here is my secret: I tell it to you with an openness of
> heart that I doubt I shall never achieve again, so I pray that you
> are in a quiet room as you read these words. My secret is that
> I need God, that I am sick and can no longer make it alone. I

need God to help me give, because I no longer seem capable of giving; to help me be kind, as I no longer seem capable of kindness; to help me love, as I seem beyond being able to love." [9]

This means that we come to church because we are *expected* to be there. We too often forget that Jesus associated with sinners and misfits, and so naturally he *was* expecting us. "I have not come to call the righteous, but sinners." (Mark 2:17) Our attitude is that we're there not to be seen, not to fulfill an obligation, but because we have been called, because we have a shared sense of need. We're there because we know that things are not as they should be in our lives, but that God cares for us anyway as we are—like the AA people down in the basement on Tuesday nights. We go to church to be reminded that whatever the ups and downs of life, we are held in the dependable relationship and unblinking gaze of the One who holds us.

One mother sums it up: "I do not impress anyone at church...I am not special at church, and this is the point...we are all equally beloved children of God...I have come to sit next to people, well aware of all we don't have in common, and face together in the same direction...Church is a group of broken individuals united only by our brokenness travelling together to ask to be fixed... Church isn't an escape from the world. It's a continuation of it. My family and I do not go to church to deny the existence of darkness. We go to look so hard at the light that our eyes water." [10]

We need to examine our motives and attitudes in coming to church. If we come to church with a deep consciousness of our shared brokenness; if we come to church because we see it as our recovery group in Jesus; if we come to church because we believe Jesus took the power of sin and evil, pain and death and made them, no longer the last words but put them next to the last words which are *forgiveness and everlasting love*; if we come to church because of the bread blessed and shared; if we come to church to be a witnessing and supporting assembly, *then* coming to church would be easier to do. It would be treasured, not endured.

Discussion Questions

1. Do you realize that the parish church is really one of the truly democratic venues in the world? As minister Fred Craddock put it, "The most extraordinary piece of Christian furniture is the pew, which invites former strangers to sit together as family."

2. At the start of Mass the celebrant says, "Brothers and sisters, let us acknowledge our sins, and so prepare ourselves to celebrate the sacred mysteries." Do you acknowledge them? The quotation that follows might give some content to this exercise.

> "I'm tired of the lies. I hear them daily, read them nightly, and watch them before I go to bed. They are so prevalent that I have a hard time knowing what is truth and what is fiction. Do cars really make you sexy? Are diamonds forever? Is a purchase the best way to show love? Is my worth tied to my waistline and my wallet? Am I worth loving based on my productivity or stature? I know that the answer to each of these is *No*. I know that these are lies, and yet I can't help but wonder. Somehow the father of lies is seeping into my subconscious and making itself at home."

Pastoral Suggestion

At Christmas, the pastor or parish representative brings a poinsettia to all families who have lost someone during the past year. Have a special ministry (run by a shut-in, preferably) that sends a remembrance card on the first anniversary of the death.

8

LESS THAN GREAT
EXPECTATIONS

IT IS UNCOMFORTABLE TO offer criticisms about people who, with dedicated hearts, offer so generously their time and services. We are so blessed by them that we hesitate to say anything critical, but, with an eye to making "Mass Matters" a better experience, I summon the courage to pass on some things I have heard over the years.

A basic pet peeve that I frequently hear from parishioners is a functional one: They can't *hear*! You would think that this is obvious, but some parishes still have an inadequate sound system. There are dead zones in some parts of the church where people can't hear without strain, if at all. Sound is tinny, or distorted, or simply not clear. I know that sound systems are more art than science, but if we have come to proclaim/hear the Word of God then the least we can expect is that we can do so.

Right off, as Mass commences, we have some opportunities for silent pauses, but so often we blow it. We bless ourselves, make an introduction indicating that we should take time to prepare ourselves to enter the liturgy by examining our consciences and then, instantaneously and without so much as a hair's breadth, we rush to recite the "I confess" as if we were all sinless so why waste time? At the Collect which follows—the collected prayers of the assembly—the celebrant intones, "Let us pray," and *again* rushes forthwith into a rapid-fire recitation. To check this lost opportunity for pause, I always intone, "Let us pray in silence," and give it an Our Father's worth of time before reading the Church's prayer. After the homily (in the prideful hope that the congregation might want to digest some of its contents), I sit down for an Our Father plus Hail Mary period before moving onto the Creed.

The Lectors

Then there are the lectors, God bless them. They range from the terrible few to the majority of merely good and adequate people, who just get up there and read but should do better, to some select excellent proclaimers who do so with clarity, meaning, and intelligence. Alas, the last of these are too rare. The thing is that the pastor is so happy to have volunteers that, even if they can't read all that well, they're in. But so many *do* read poorly, with no sense of pause—that silence theme again—for meaning and understanding. They tend to read too rapidly and move quickly from reading to reading. Some can't be heard. Others drop words or consonants. Some voices are too thin or too indistinct.

You would think that, with all the episcopal rhetoric about proclaiming the Word of God that good, well-trained lectors would be the norm. You would think that such a vital thing as proclaiming God's Word at Sunday Mass would be top priority and only the better readers would be approved to fill this august role. Unfortunately, lectoring has become simply utilitarian.

Mindful of lectoring as a calling and the importance and dignity of the role, there should be ongoing and vigorous selection, training, and monitoring. Most lectors, dedicated as they are, would welcome the opportunity. Wouldn't it be a nice novelty, as well as sending a message about the importance of the Word, if the parish Rosary Altar society or the Knights of Columbus would fund an annual training of lectors? Perhaps several parishes could join in a common enterprise. *That* would make a statement!

At some churches, the lector actually tells the congregation where to find the readings in the missalettes so they can follow along word by word. Many do pick up the missalette containing the script and heads are bowed in a reading rather than listening mode. I don't think that the mandate of proclaiming the Word of God is quite fulfilled that way. I know there may be some who like to savor reading along with the lector as an extra way of absorbing the scripture, or maybe some of them read along because the lector is unintelligible or inaudible, but I still feel—my own opinion—that ideally the congregation is there to listen to the proclamation, not proofread the Scripture. Others will disagree with me here, but my gut instinct is to get rid of the missalettes altogether. Just have some in the vestibule for the hearing impaired, although some more progressive parishes have wisely adopted what theaters routinely do today, namely having hearing devices that can be obtained and returned to the sacristy.

Can you imagine going to a Broadway play with the script in hand and having your head buried in its pages all during the performance? Can you imagine the dynamics of the sets, the lights, the music, and the actors all bypassed? Why do we encourage a congregation to read along with Jack or Jill instead of encouraging listening intently to a well-proclaimed word that, at the end, we boldly declare to have been "The Word of the Lord"? It is interesting that almost every parish in the US hands out the "Workbook for Lectors, Gospel Readers, and Proclaimers of the Word" put out by Liturgy Training Publications. The workbook contains all the readings of a given liturgical year with commentaries at the bottom and guidelines and technique suggestions on the sidebar to make the lectors more effective. You'll find such things as phonetic spellings for difficult names and places, advice on the nature of the reading, and practical suggestions such as "smile to make the reading more attractive," "pause after this line," "stress certain words" "convey the crowd's excitement," " raise your voice here," and so on. The one I'm interested in is this bit of advice: "Making eye contact with the assembly connects you with them and connects them to the reading more deeply than using your voice alone. This helps the assembly stay with the story and keeps them engaged." Eye contact is hard to do if the lector is looking at 400 scalps. So, to coax the people away from reading and on to listening, we need well-trained lectors.

The Music

As far as music goes, there is much admiration for the cantors and choirs who give of their time and talent to praise God. There is, however, as I have discovered over the years, sometimes a very thin line between enhancement and entertainment, between background (like subtle gorgeous movie music) and the whole show. While some hymns are carefully thought out and much music is appropriate, too often they both slip into television hype. I've been in parishes where the closing hymn is a rallying, over-the-top crescendo with the musician or singer's final trills practically begging for applause. And it happens. At every Mass the congregation, Sunday after Sunday, applauds the choir or contemporary folk group at the end. They don't applaud the ushers or altar servers or lectors, and not even the celebrant who may have given a stirring homily. The applause for grandstanding music that suffocates the Mass is misplaced. There *are* times when applause is called for, but they should be few and far between. Bottom line: When the music dominates rather than supports the liturgy, we *are* into entertainment.

After the readings comes the homily—but that needs its own chapter later. Right now, we need to move on to the next chapter to explore the world of whisperers and waiters and other assorted ministers.

Discussion Questions

1. How's the sound system in your parish? Are there "dead" spots"? Does it offer hearing aids for the hearing impaired?
2. How, generally, is the quality of the lectors in your parish? On a scale of 1 to 10, with 10 being the highest praise, how would you rate them? Explain.
3. How is the music in your parish? Does it enhance or distract?
4. Do the people sing? Does the music minister teach you appropriate hymns until you know them well enough to sing?
5. How can you make the parish more welcoming to others?

Pastoral Suggestion

Most parishes have some form of outreach to the poor and needy. On the last Sunday of the month, we asked people to bring food or necessities to Mass and place them in the sanctuary (involve the children). After the last Mass of the month—we let the visual stand for all Masses—we would have pre-assigned families or individuals approach the sanctuary, pick up a bundle and lead the procession out of church to our Sharing Shed after this prayer:

> Almighty God, lover of the poor and friend of the outcast, bless those who gave this food from the goodness of their hearts. Bless, too, the hands that will receive it. And may all of us know that, as disciples of the Lord and servants to one another, we are but doing our duty beholden as we are to the gospel of Our Lord Jesus Christ.

The carriers are sprinkled with holy water and then process out.

9

MASS ETIQUETTE

THE CREED IS A late addition to the history of the Mass. We have both the Apostles' Creed, whose origins go back to the first century, and the Nicene Creed that goes back to the fourth century. Although we mostly use the Nicene Creed, the Apostles' Creed may be used at Advent and Lent—and I wish more parishes would take advantage of this option. The words of the Nicene Creed are archaic, but the creed is well placed at the beginning of our Eucharistic celebration and it reminds us of the ancientness of the faith. It tells us that we are a Universal Church united with all those countless other believers, who this very day will recite these same beliefs and break the same bread—and, for some of them, as we noted, at the risk of their lives.

After the Creed comes the Prayers of the Faithful. They were encouraged by Vatican II as a way of assuring our catholicity, that is, that we pray for the world, not just our own preoccupations; these include prayers for the Church in general, public authorities, and local needs. Many are good. Some are too wordy. Some stray as we are asked to pray for Aunt Minnie's safe trip or that the Vikings win. I'm always amused when the lector instructs, "Our response is, 'Lord, hear our prayer'." When *isn't* that the response? Since 99% of the time it is, save the instruction for when it varies.

Mass continues, and we come to the Consecration and my comment here, I admit, is a personal idiosyncratic observation readily disregarded. It is this. Even as a child, I would see the priest celebrant gear himself up as he approached the Consecration. He would back up, lean way over, place his forearms on the altar table, and then bent over with eyes riveted on the bread or the chalice, whisper into them the words of consecration as if he were talking to some little people we couldn't see. It was almost like a private conversation up there. I suppose that, for the centuries-old "private" Mass celebrated alone as a private devotion—an oxymoron now and generally prohibited—it might have made some sense, but it does not make sense now.

I just can't imagine that's the way Jesus did it. Did he really take the unleavened bread and then the cup, bend way over them so that he lost eye contact and whispered, "Take this, all of you"? I can imagine the disciples saying, "What? We can't hear you," or, pulling a Robert de Niro and asking, "Are you talking to me?" Well, I'm being irreverent. But Jesus obviously took the bread and cup and, clearly with great deliberation, because he was changing something in the usual ritual, looked directly at his disciples and said, "Take this," and handed it to them- a gesture that needed face-to-face contact. It was a straightforward momentous action.

Think of yourselves. You baked special bread for your guests. So, you hunch over the bread plate, lean on your elbows, and talk to the bread in a solemn voice, "You really ought to try this bread. I made it myself. It's delicious!" No, you pointedly pick the bread up, show it to your guests, and you look at them in the eye and say your piece. It always seemed to me that that's the way to do it at Mass: take the bread and, later, the chalice, show them to the congregation and then speak to your intended audience—not to the bread and wine. Look at the people solemnly and prayerfully, which is only the natural thing to do when you're telling someone to take this or that. I want to add that I realize and appreciate what is happening. It's an attempt to show special reverence for this solemn moment: the lowering of the voice, the bow, the eyes averted to the species. I respect that, but it just seems to me not quite true to the art of such profound Gift-giving.

Cleanup Time

Okay, back to the Mass. We come to Communion and, before my testy comments, it's good to remember two things. First, recalling that we are the assembly of the broken, we quote Pope Francis who reminds us that Communion is not some grand prize for the perfect person but rather food for the hungry one. Second, what is physically and symbolically happening is that we are approaching the altar with an empty hand and accepting what the priest offers: the Eucharistic Jesus. *We are coming down that aisle in profound need and dependency*. At the same time, our being there to join this Communion pilgrimage makes the statement that we have also turned away, for the moment, from worldly activities—the TV watching back home, the newspapers, the football game—and taking time for God. Okay, here is a little thing and no one is probably thinking these thoughts, but maybe the next time you go to Communion they might kick in. You might remember, like a child in need, why you are there doing what you're doing.

Picture that moment after Communion when everything is being put away and, alas, the exit begins; this provokes a few more curmudgeon grumbles, one of them being, for heaven's sake, do the dishes *after* the guests have gone! I don't know of any other civilization that has you to dinner and makes you sit while the hosts bring over the basin and water and do the dishes before they serve dessert and coffee. Yet that is what often happens at the Eucharistic banquet: the celebrant or deacons doing the dishes while you wait for dismissal. Lord help the congregation if it gets a priest or deacon afflicted with the "theology of the crumb" and you sit there impatiently while he vigorously scours and wipes and wipes and re-wipes every vessel lest a little bit of Jesus be leftover. Clean up *after* Mass!

So, we're ready to depart with a summary prayer and a communal send-off hymn in our hearts. But, as the TV commercials say, "But wait! Before you go, we have a few announcements," and they are the last things we hear before we go. So, the moment is trivialized, and the mood is altered as, ready to depart, we sit for announcements that are already in the bulletin. Which makes you think about why we even have the bulletins at all. Announcements are a nervousness that afflicts pastors. Then there are some announcements, most notably any changed or sudden events but this should be a brief and rare occasion, not a routine one. Certainly, announcements should not exceed four in number, yet I have sat through anywhere from five to twelve of them.

One simple solution I have discovered in a parish where I was helping out: announcements were made right after the Prayers of the Faithful. Brilliant! As soon as those prayers are over, the congregation always sits down, the people begin to reach for their purses or wallets or envelopes and the ushers start down the aisles to move from front to back to take up the collection. Eventually the gifts bearers begin to line up. Meanwhile, during this routine transition time between the two parts of the Mass, a time of comfortable and necessary distraction, the announcements are delivered and over with by the time the gift bearers have assembled to precede the ushers, laden with the collection, to the sanctuary. It's such a natural and unobtrusive time to make announcements. Another parish emails the parish bulletin to every registered family each Monday.

The thing is that people today are literate and computer savvy. It's a matter of training them to take home the bulletin that should be given out *after* Mass, not given to them beforehand as casual reading *during* Mass. After missing some good stuff—plus having some terrific timely things in the bulletin—people will learn to do so. Besides, you can post announcements in the vestibule or, again, online. Most parishes have web pages.

Allied with this, be parsimonious about solicitations or recruiting. I know the noble organizations of Rosary- Altar or Men's Guild need members, but to end Mass with announcements and then an appeal for new members or programs once more dissipates the liturgical experience. It's like giving a magnificent lecture only to be followed by some clown who tells really funny jokes. The audience leaves laughing, but not many will remember the talk.

The idea is that, if you've had a good liturgy—good reading, good homily, good music—let these linger. Close off the liturgy with a song, not a commercial. The Mass should be a whole. From the greeting at the beginning to the closing hymn at the end, there should be no detours however interesting or entertaining they may be.

Way back, someone succinctly summed up the experience of going to church this way:

> Gather the folk
> Tell the story
> Break the Bread
> Share the experience.

Discussion Questions

1. I'm aware that this chapter has contained an eccentric list of negative comments. I thought of entitling it, "Picky, Picky!" Anyway, do *you* have things that bother you or distract you when you go to church?
2. More to the point, for you, what are the very positive things about going to church? What are the things you like, and the things that make you happy that you came to church?

Pastoral Suggestion

Single people, young or old, are often unintentionally marginalized in the parish. The parish can offer a ministry geared to them. It can also watch out for the subtle signals. We would never have a parish dance that, say, cost $10.00 a couple but rather $5.00 per person. Singles would be invited to take on a liturgical ministry just for one month, for example, as altar server, usher, or lector—enough to publicly recognize their presence and value.

10

HEARD ANY GOOD
HOMILIES LATELY?

ST PAUL **ONCE PREACHED** so long that one of his listeners, Eutychus, fell asleep and fell from an upper window and died. Paul of course, being Paul, raised him up. Whether the man was grateful or not is not recorded (Acts 20:7-14).

Complaints about preaching go way back, which is why it gets its own chapter. In almost every poll taken, poor preaching ranks way, way up among the disenchantments with the Catholic Church. A recent survey from the Pew Research Center shows that the quality of sermons is the single most important factor in attracting people to church. Poor preaching simply drives people away. They either stay home or travel to other denominations. One of the practical differences between Protestants and Catholics is that good preaching is an essential factor in ordaining ministers while in the Catholic church good ritual is the essential factor in ordaining priests. The focal point in Protestant churches is the pulpit; in the Catholic Church, the altar.

The difference shows. You go to a Protestant church and *expect* to get good preaching. Go to a Catholic Church, and it's a roll of the dice. That's the truth. To be sure the bishops have put out tons of documents, exhortations, guidelines, and pastoral letters about the necessity of good preaching, but, deep down, they are not serious. All talk and no action. They are not serious because they do nothing about poor preaching. They will not ordain one who can't explain transubstantiation, for example, but *will* ordain a candidate who is a poor preacher. The bishops are subconsciously acting like they're back in the medieval ages when the Catholic Church had a monopoly on salvation and so preaching didn't matter because you had a captive audience who had to be there anyway if they wanted to be saved. I understand the bishops are constrained by the severe priest shortage. They're glad to have a warm body to ascend the pulpit at all. But that's not a good enough excuse. It's not good enough because bad, boring, dreadful and, at times, spiritually harmful preaching starves the Church and impedes evangelization.

I know further that the bishops are not serious about preaching because there is not, and never has been, a system, a mechanism to monitor preaching. Think of it. No corporation would let loose a salesperson who stutters, a surgeon who trembles, an actor who forgets, or a candidate who has no platform. Yet we allow anyone, as long as he doesn't deny the Trinity, to preach regardless of his ability to do so.

Good preaching is essential, so much so that a big hitter, a famous theologian of the twentieth century, Yves Conger, once said, "I could quote a whole series of ancient texts all saying more or less the same thing, that if in one country's Mass was celebrated for thirty years without preaching and in another there was preaching without the Mass, people would be more Christian in the country where there was preaching." He's absolutely right.

You would think that with the severe decline of religion in general and of the Catholic Church in particular, and where there are more ex-Catholics than there are Presbyterians, that the bishops would tend more to the basic ward unit of the church, the parish, and especially its preaching, since again that stands so high as a chief complaint where it is bad and a chief draw where it is good.

The Foreign Priest

Then there are the foreign priests. Ah, yes. As we shall see, they are and will be more commonly the face of the Church. We are grateful for them. We need them. In many cases we love them but can't understand a word they say in the pulpit. Again, imagine going to church and not understanding one word the preacher said. It's worse than going to a foreign movie with no subtitles. You just sit there and, for the searchers or those in desperate need of an enlightening or comforting word, what a frustration, what an emptiness! Again Amazon, Costco, and your local Stop & Shop would never tolerate such a lack of communication.

Whoops, I'm getting cynical. Sorry, it's just that I feel bad for the people looking for nourishment and coming away hungry. It's not that as a preacher myself I don't relate to the difficulty of coming up every week with a homily, not to mention wedding, funeral, and sacramental celebrations in between. I know that these are days of a priest shortage. Priests are overworked, often serving several parishes. Gone are the days of having associates. There are endless meetings, visitations, and other time-consuming necessities to keep the parish afloat.

Still, I remain envious of our Protestant brothers and sisters who begin their preparations Monday morning, and I bemoan that we have no tradition of doing this; that unlike our Protestant brothers and sisters, we have no tradition of absolutely sacred time, *well-known and well-respected in the parish*, when the minister is not to be disturbed. He's preparing his sermon. Well, more lay involvement is surely one answer. Another answer is for a parish to consciously create that sacred space for the priest. Protect this well-known sacred time in the interest of good preaching.

Solutions

Meanwhile, let me get back to the foreign priest. Let him audition before a group of mentors. Where his English is bad, send him to class until he is good enough, certified, if you will, to preach. After all, it is unkind to him and distressful to the people to let him ascend the pulpit otherwise. Think of yourself speaking in a foreign country in a language not native to you! Post his homily on the parish website if his wise words are worth hearing. Meanwhile, let well-spoken deacons substitute. Let me press on by suggesting that, for the preached homily, substitute a recording or a video of an engaging and approved speaker. You might then coordinate this with discussion questions in the Sunday bulletin. I know it sounds weird. There's nothing like a live preacher, but in desperate times where, again, the homily is so key in attracting or distancing people, what would you rather have: a recorded nourishing homily that is well-preached, or a live one that rambles, or one you can't hear or understand? Bishops, think it over.

Finally, let's get bolder. In the case of poor or hard to understand homilies, what about lay people preaching? Seeing that the stakes are so high, it's got to come to that sooner or later. Canon Law (225) says, "In those circumstances in which people can hear the gospel and know Christ only through lay persons," the laity has an obligation to spread the gospel. Why could these words not extend to lay preachers? It might have happened in the early Church but was quickly relegated to the office of bishop and priest and then became law at the Council of Trent. Today, however, the universal call to holiness and the new competence of the lay people make that worth a second look. In 1988, the US Bishops allowed lay people to preach at retreats, revivals, missions, and large gatherings of the faithful, although not at Mass. Canon Law (225) does recognize the obligation of the laity to spread the gospel. These days when lay people are pastoring parishes the question has become more urgent.

In fact, in July of 2018, the Commission known as ARCIC III, the Anglican-Roman Catholic International Communion, seeking reunion issued a new ground-breaking statement that restored ecumenical dialogue after a hiatus caused by the changes within the Anglican Communion, such as the priestly and episcopal ordination of women.

The new statement, called "Walking Together on the Way: Learning to Be the Church—Local, Regional, Universal," overcomes obstacles to dialogue by inviting Catholics and Anglicans to learn from each other's differences rather than focusing on what each has in common. Anglicans are encouraged, for instance, to learn about models of unity from the Catholic Church, while Catholics are invited to consider how the laity can be better involved in decision-making. One interesting paragraph suggests that ecumenism might advance if the Catholic Church considered women deacons, married priests, and lay preachers. It says, "While the commission recognizes that some decisions regarding ministry made by provinces of the Anglican Communion are not open to the Roman Catholic community, others potentially are, e.g. a female diaconate (which would automatically open up preaching to women); a fuller implementation of licensed lay pastoral assistants; the priestly ordination of mature married men—*viri probati*; and the authorization of laypeople to preach." So, the Spirit is moving.

Children of This Age

In the middle of 2018, the giant company, Starbucks, had a crisis. It seems that one of their many franchises had shown discrimination against two black customers. In the prevailing climate, that was like touching the third rail. Immediately, Starbucks shut down all its stores nationwide and made its staff take a two-day sensitivity training. You can't have a brand name with a bad name. It's bad for business.

Question: Can you imagine the local diocese doing this for a deficient parish or offensive pastor? Not in your or my lifetime, or ever.

All of which proves that Jesus was right when he commented, "The children of this age are more shrewd in dealing with their own generation than are the children of the light." (Luke 16:8). So, leaving aside major catastrophes like the clergy abuse scandals and their cover-ups, when *was* the last time a diocese took action against clergy or parishes that fell short of their mission and drove people away? The Church, unlike the big secular companies, has never had what we might call an ongoing quality check for its parishes or clergy. Outside of assiduously sniffing out heresy, it never had what we might call a pastoral quality control department, a kind of diocesan Red Cross. I am not implying a Gestapo-like police force that enforces rigidity and promotes fear, but an official professional pastoral group of people who caringly respond to local misdemeanors, mismanagement, offensive policies, alienating leadership, or poor liturgies. With Starbucks-like urgency, they are there not to condemn but to offer help, retraining, and support. Embrace those last three words.

It seems reasonable to ask that, given the obvious need, why has this never taken place? The answer again is because the Church is still operating on an obsolete and counterproductive theology of Church as a "perfect" society. After all, we have been taught, it is One, Holy, Catholic, Apostolic and, at one point, Indefectible. It operates according to Pope Boniface VII's dictum "outside the church there is no salvation." You had to go to church no matter what you found there. Custom, a strong faith, social pressure, fear of hell, the Church billed as the "one true Church—these assumptions prevailed and kept the faithful coming regardless of what went on. Let me hasten to say that "what went on" was often wonderful and meaningful. Nevertheless, whether the liturgy was meaningful or meaningless, the preacher effective or insipid, parish policies fair or fickle, the pastor shepherd or wolf—all were ultimately irrelevant. You needed the Church to be saved. The Church had a monopoly on salvation and the laity needed its rituals and sacraments to make it happen. Live with it.

Hello! Has anyone noticed that today is different? That, for better or for worse, we have a people who are educated, empowered, enamored of personal freedom, dedicated to equality and choice, imbued with a high sense of individualism and a low sense of community loyalty. "Children of the light" should take this into consideration and firmly but gently provide a system to fix what is broken.

Let me end on the sour note that sometimes the people are not entirely blameless. So often, it seems, some consider a good preacher to be the one who entertains best (the media impact): you know, great jokes, references to the latest rock band and popular movies, one who dazzles the crowd—and, above all, is brief! In short, he's a "personality." Whether there's any substance there is another question.

Okay, let's lighten up with some slings and arrows directed at us preachers:

> I cannot praise the reverend's eyes/I never saw his glance divine/He always shuts them when he prays/And when he preaches, he shuts mine!

> Comedian George Burns: "A good sermon should have a good beginning and a good ending, and they should be as close together as possible."

A little girl became restless as the preacher's sermon dragged on and on. Finally, she leaned over to her mother and whispered, "Mommy, if we give him the money now, will he let us go?"

A preacher is one who talks in other people's sleep. (Ouch!)

Discussion Questions

1. How would you rate your parish preaching in general?
2. Do you praise the priest/deacon when his preaching is good and encourage him when less so?
3. What do you think of the suggestions for dealing with the beloved but hard-to-understand foreign priest?
4. Would you be open to laypeople preaching? Why or why not?

Pastoral Suggestion

People live busy (and stressful) lives these days. They don't have much time to volunteer in the parish. Besides, some are afraid that if they do, they're caught forever. You know, you come in for a Mass card and wind up head of the Rosary-Altar society. To counter this, we instituted a "one-shot-piggyback deal". That is to say, the people get a personal letter from the pastor (he still has some clout and they discover they are known!) You ask them, if possible, to do one simple specific thing, say, serve the coffee and donuts after Mass or help pack food baskets for Thanksgiving. It's a one-shot event, not forever. Someone will guide them and when they're done, they simply pass on the experience to the next volunteer. I have found that many people are appreciative they're not signing up for a career as a church worker, find the experience pleasant, and they are apt to volunteer for other things. At least their parish anonymity has been blown and they really do appreciate the fact that they have been recognized.

11

THE RAINBOW CHURCH

WHEN I WAS GROWING up, my neighborhood parish church had a fair mix of nationalities represented. The number of African-American Catholics was relatively small, so it was a combination of mostly white Europeans with a smaller number of Asians, Hispanics, and mid-east Catholics. Today, in a new era of declining white membership and expanding migration, the proportions have reversed dramatically. This is so much so that I venture to say that in many sections of the country—my own at least—almost every parish now has a Spanish Mass. This means that these days, whether you get to the church on time or not, you will notice, beyond the more frequent foreign clergy, the rainbow effect in both the ministers and in the pews. It's not predominately whites in church anymore. In fact, to make two very emphatic points, ponder these: by the middle of this century, non-Hispanic whites will be in a minority in the US. In 2013, for the first time ever, most US infants under the age of one were non-white.

All this came home to me about a dozen years ago when I began to celebrate weekend Mass at a wonderful little church called Holy Innocents. It was right up the highway from the large local hospital. Many of the hospital workers came from India, the Philippines, Asia, Mexico, the Caribbean Islands, and other similar countries. They were good and devout churchgoers. What impressed and excited me was not only the rainbow congregation spread out before me but the absolute total color blindness of the congregation. People of all stripes knew each other, greeted, chatted, joked, and hugged one another like the spiritual family it was. Now that was a *Catholic* church!

Such a composite is becoming the norm.

Let's backtrack a bit and put things in perspective. First, we in the US tend to think that *we're* the center of the ecclesiastical universe. It may come as a surprise to learn that there are about 1.3 *billion* Catholics in the world, but of this only 70 million are in the United States. *This means that we represent less than six percent of the global Catholic population.* Yet many of us thought we were the whole show among those foreigners who lived somewhere else! We may be the richest part of the Church, but we are far from the largest and the Pope has a lot more to worry about globally than our relatively minor domestic needs. This in turn means that we have to be a bit more humble and realize that our evaluations, priorities, opinions, experiences, interests, and politics are not necessarily those of the rest of the world. We cannot always set the tone or think the Church is us.

A Country of Immigrants

Secondly, we have forgotten that ours has always been a country of immigrants. Most of us come from immigrant parents, grandparents, or great grandparents. My father was born in New Jersey, but his parents were born in Germany. My mother was born in Italy. Millions of European immigrants arrived in this country in the 19th and 20th centuries. These immigrants, inelegantly dubbed the PIGS—Poles, Irish/Italian, Germans, and Slovaks—were vehemently despised by the Protestant majority because they were mostly from Catholic countries and subject to fierce nativist prejudice. A common sign outside employment offices in the East was "Dogs & Irish Need Not Apply." The Catholics tended to settle in mainly two regions, the Northeast and the Midwest, where our ancestors, with great determination and sacrifice and much opposition, built a huge network of parishes, schools, hospitals, and social services equal to that of the government, eventually making the Catholic Church the largest denomination in the country. That may be hard to believe in today's reality of shrinking numbers. Since Catholics did mostly settle in the Northeast and Midwest, that's where most of our parishes, schools, colleges, universities, seminaries, hospitals, and publishing companies are located. This is news to those of us born and raised in the East and West enclaves.

Thirdly, and this is critical, we do not appreciate that not only are we currently experiencing a new wave of immigrants, but also that they are largely Catholic and come not from Europe, but mostly from that other America: South America. In fact, "others" are increasingly the American church. Today in the US, there are more than 4,000 foreign-born religious sisters. Roughly one-fourth of all diocesan priests come from foreign countries, and three in ten American priests ordained in 2016 were born outside the country. [11]

The stats: In 1965 there were 48.5 million Catholics in the US. Fifty years later, there were 75 million—and this takes into account the millions who have left the Church. The difference was the arrival of the Hispanic people. They now account for 71 percent of the Catholic population and are mostly settled in the Southwest. But note, it's not all a question of immigration. Two thirds of Hispanics were born here. No surprise since they *are* the oldest group in the land. About half of them identify as Catholic. In fact, the majority of US Catholics under age eighteen are Hispanic. Think about that and what it means for the future.

Okay, that's the bird's eye view, the way things are. The practical reality means that going to church has also come to mean metaphorically going to church at this time, that is, at this moment of history. It is clear that we must rearrange our priorities and set aside any nativist feelings we may have. Remember that, at one time, the slow, steady amalgamation of our ancestors made us one Church in America. Whatever we did has to be repeated—and pretty much in the same (uphill) way. To start off with, we need to recruit more Hispanic priests, deacons, lay ecclesial ministers, and religious. We need as much effort, money, and time for them as we put into formerly "standard" candidates.

We need to welcome the Hispanic people and, yes, even evangelize them because the sad news is that about one out of four of them is a former Catholic and defections are increasing each year.

Most young Hispanics left before age twenty-four, giving reasons that ranged from just drifting away, stopped believing in the teachings of their childhood religion, marriage to an evangelical, to the complaint that they desired "a direct, personal experience of God and did not experience it at the local parish." That is why forty-three percent of the drifters call themselves "born-again" and why the Pew Forum on Religion and Public Life could speculate that while "more than two-thirds of the 52 million-plus Latinos in the US are Catholic, that number could be cut in half by 2030."

What I'm saying is that we need to embrace and accommodate the Hispanic culture and incorporate the Hispanic people. They have a rich expressive, cultural background. Our cerebral Mass doesn't always speak to them. As one Hispanic lady who joined an evangelical church said, "I found that when I went to the Catholic Church, it was like they were reading a book. But at my church it is like I feel the Holy Spirit wrapping his arms around me." Our private restrained devotions pale next to their colorful communal embrace of Our Lady of Guadalupe. They are strongly drawn to our native Charismatic Renewal. They are susceptible to the close-knittedness and the appeal of the Pentecostal churches. Many South American countries, in fact, have already measurably stopped identifying as being Catholic and have moved to being identified as Pentecostal. In some places they still go to Mass, but afterwards they go to the Pentecostal gatherings.

Giving Welcome

These facts merit repeating a prior observation. As I mentioned previously, the Post Vatican II liturgical renewals were left in the hands of the head people, the intellectuals who were focused on orthodoxy. In the drive to renew the Mass, they gave short shrift, with a touch of snobbery, to popular devotions that had overshadowed the Mass. There was certainly need for a cleansing as some folkloric religion, at times, bordered on magic and the superstitious. I remember as a young priest being put in charge of the parish Bingo. (I hated it.) I was scandalized seeing some of the women using miraculous medals as markers! There was a point: all those rosaries during Mass, statues, scapulars, visions, appearances, and some dubious ethnic practices deflected from "full and active participation" in the Mass. There surely was need for setting priorities. But in the process, the reformers went too far and the devotional life of the Church declined. People became too embarrassed for that sort of thing and, consequently, the great hallmark of the Church, the Catholic Imagination, floundered. Where are our Catholic artists, sculptors, and authors today?

The irony is that the secular world is replete with ritual, symbols, popular art, and, universally, music. Look at the logoed T-shirts, the brands of the six-billion-dollar franchised football teams, the stereotyped "vestments" of rock stars, the flowers left at places of tragedy, and the merchandizing of everything. We have to admit that the Mass, while the apex, is simply not enough. People need integrated faith expressions and symbols. We need to welcome the new face of the Church with an imagination beyond our Anglo-Saxon confines. We need to listen to the Hispanic people, learn from them, recruit them, and learn to celebrate what they celebrate. More and more, they're sitting next to us in the pews. More and more, they are us.

A Cautionary Tale

As so often in our past, the increased arrival of Hispanics has raised nativist concerns. "Why can't they come here legally and learn to speak English? My grandparents did. Let them have their own parishes or Masses." It's an old problem. Our country's history is full of previous immigrants distaining and discriminating against new waves of immigrants. Famously, for example, the Irish were subject to vicious animosity when they came to America fleeing the potato famine of their homeland in the 1840's. They had to compete with the German Americans, but, in time, they so dominated the East Coast Church that by 1880s, in Boston for example, eighty percent of the clergy was Irish and eventually most of the hierarchy was also.

When the Italians came, there was strong antipathy between the two—competing for jobs, for example: the Italians were willing to work for lower pay—and turf wars both in and out of the Church were common. Martin Scorsese's 2002 film, "The Gangs of New York," powerfully reflects the tensions. Later, the dominant Irish encountered immigrants from Poland and other Eastern European countries. This created more tensions and conflicts, so much so that the bishops decided to create "separate but equal" national parishes. Still, the hostility continued to such an extent that some Poles founded their own renegade Catholic Church in Scranton, Pennsylvania and so did the Lithuanians and Slovaks. Alarmed, eventually the bishops no longer would allow national churches.

In the Southwest, Mexicans experienced severe discrimination among the Catholics. They often had to sit in the last pews. The point is that every new wave of immigrants has found itself excluded or marginalized, not only in society at large but also often in church. Today, as we are living in times of great waves of immigration with all of its problems, we must be alert to any tensions between native-born Catholics and the new Catholic immigrants. As heirs to the One who was once an immigrant in Egypt and who said, "Come to me, all of you who are weary and burdened and I will give you rest" (Matt. 11:28-30), we must give them welcome.

Finally, let us note that, beyond the Catholic spiritual kinship with Latinos, the same spirit of welcome and toleration should be extended to the Muslims whose numbers have now expanded to nearly four million in our country. A 2018 Pew Survey predicts that by 2040 Muslims will replace Jews as the nation's second-largest religious group after Christians.

By 2050, the US Muslim population is projected to reach 8.1 million, or 2.1% of the nation's total population—nearly twice the number of today. Hampered by the excesses of their radical extremists and the nativist suspicion of the outsider, they suffer considerable discrimination.

No one baptized in the name of Christ Jesus should be a part of that.

Discussion Questions

Worth noting: Hispanics, conservative in religion but liberal in politics, are quicker to gather and create social movements to improve their life conditions, including such issues as immigration status and gender equality. While quicker to believe in the miraculous, they are also much more willing to bend ecclesiastical rules. How can we harness these qualities?

Pastoral Suggestions

Even in past decades, we could see the growing Hispanic presence and so our marvelous music ministry would introduce Spanish hymns and teach them to the congregation. A congregation who once learned by heart the "Tantum ergo" and "O Solitaris" had no trouble learning them and singing them as part of the usual repertoire.

Pastors might alert their people (via the bulletin or homily?) to the story of 89-year-old Father Jacques Hamel who, in 2016, was celebrating Mass in Normandy when two men, armed with knives and claiming allegiance to the Islamic State, charged in and slit his throat. The event sent shock waves throughout France and elsewhere. Fr. Hamel had been a close friend of the local Imam with whom he had organized interfaith dialogues. *Muslims across France attended Mass to show their solidarity*. Not all Muslims are extremists.

12

CANTANKEROUS COMMENTS

WE'VE COME TO THE end of our commonly themed chapters and you can profitably stop reading here because I've made the main points I wanted to make. Sometimes, however, like baking a pie or building a bird house, I've got some pieces left over, pieces that, I confess, amount to little more than an opinionated potpourri of free-ranging commentary—mixed with comments people have laid on me over the years—with which you may disagree and argue over, but, before we move on to the next section, if you have nothing better to do, reading this might be better than watching television.

Cycling the Bible

The liturgical purists, buoyed by Vatican II, have given new life to the homily: we preachers should preach on the scriptures, and the people should hear it in its fullness. To this end, the liturgists revised the lectionary so that most of the Bible is read in a three-year cycle. There would be three readings for Sundays and two for the weekdays. Thus, the Catholic population, it was argued, so exposed to the Word of God as never before, in a three-year cycle would become biblically literate. Well, I don't know if that last phrase was explicit but, in any case, the experiment has largely failed. The idea is good, but in practice it doesn't work out that way. For one thing, omitted from the cycle are the books of Obadiah, Judith, 1 Chronicles, plus only a smidgen or two citations from the Song of Songs (too hot to handle) and other passages too difficult to parse. In fact, someone has calculated, in that three-year cycle people will hear only about fifteen percent of the Old Testament and about forty-five percent of the New Testament. Anyway, to get the full import of this arrangement, people would have to go to Mass *daily* as well as on Sundays. The fact is those long weekday readings, say, from Maccabees or Daniel, are never heard by the vast majority of the weekend Mass goers.

The first reading from the Old Testament is designed to be related to the gospel in a kind of promise-fulfillment parallel. It often works out that way, but sometimes those two readings plus the epistle, unless you have your degree in Sanskrit, Egyptology, or Biblical Studies, defy connections for the ordinary person. The effort to do so often tends to be a bit strained and artificial as the homilist tries to make them connect. ("Well, as we heard in the first reading and then in St. Paul, the gospel....") As liturgist Father Joe Nolan wrote a while back, "It's time to say that people standing up to read dense passages from the book of Kings—or whatever—is simply a business of going through the motions." Add to this St. Paul's sometimes-tortured interpretations and you join his contemporary, St. Peter, who complained that he had no clue as to what Paul was talking about.

I think the idea of the three readings is good in theory, but I wonder if it works in practice. For example, it is axiomatic that, after all the years of conditioning by around-the-clock staccato commercials and sound-bite newscasts, the public's attention span has shrunk. Teachers are acutely aware of the notoriously short attention span of students who see the world through quick camera cuts. People are used to short single-issue focused messages hammered over and over again. Think of all those numbing commercials. Therefore, to offer the people at Mass three discrete readings with three distinct messages or points—remember, people really do not always see the connections that scholars do—plus the homily, and hope that the people will retain all of them doesn't cut it even if they could understand them. Add to this the occasional gospel that contains two totally different messages and you have overload. Still, even if the people understand what they view as four messages, for the modern mind such messages, heard in a short time, this doesn't seem to be where a mediatized people are. Yes, I concede that ideally the preacher's task is to harmonize the three readings, but how often does that happen? You have to either presume the congregation has a certain level of biblical literacy or, in a short ten minutes, try to harmonize them.

I am willing to bet that most people at Mass, including the celebrant, can't even remember five minutes after Mass what the first two readings were. (Ask yourself: Do I?) What I'm saying is that I'm not sure the three-year cycle and the connections get through. Maybe we need to remind the people now and then of their meaning and purpose and connectivity. One thing I feel sure of is that it's time to redo the three cycles of readings in a more coherent way, this time with pastoral people (and poets) at the experts' sides. I confess that I have sometimes thought that replacing one or other scripture excerpts with some compatible and exquisite spiritual readings from recognized spiritual masters past and present, readings that people can understand, relate to, remember, and take home might be the way to go. I'm definitely in the minority here.

Homilies versus sermons

When I was assigned my first pastorate, it was in the heady and confusing days of post-Vatican II when everyone was floundering with its new (actually ancient) concepts of collegiality, identity, Mass changes, and so on. I knew it couldn't be business as usual with the newly commanded scripture-based "homily." The people first needed a period of adjustment to learn how to become "Church." As St. Paul said, "How can they call on him they have not believed? And how can they believe in him of whom they have not heard? And how can they hear without someone to preach" (Romans 10:14-15)? *The people* needed to be prepped to call on Jesus. *I* needed to empower them, not in the sense of sharing my or the bishop's power, but in the sense of acknowledging the power they *already* had in virtue of their baptism. They were not my children. Rather, each of us having different gifts, they were my peers and collaborators and we had to build on that reality.

So, I began a process that lasted about four to five years. I preached practical sermons, not scriptural homilies. We went over again and again *who* they were, *why* they were, and *how* they were as a People of God. That was the stuff of my sermons. I tried to help them see God's universal call to holiness, their own charisms, and their calling as adult Christians. I wanted them to feel that they were indeed a People of God, and that, as I told them, I would leave someday but they would remain as the local Church who had all the fullness of the universal Church. They were *not* just a franchise of the Vatican. In addition to my sermons, every Sunday I had people insert material into the bulletin which I took from the best writers concerning Vatican II. I gave lectures on the changes and the reasons behind them, why some were good, some bad. My favorite mantra was "shared and collaborative ministry" meaning "we worked together, were Church together." I encouraged independence in that they didn't need permission to do good. I hired a full-time spiritual director, and what a difference that made as many people became conversant with the great saints and mystics. I was preparing them to hear the scriptures—the homily—with adult minds and hearts.

Yes, yes, I was supposed to preach on the gospel, but I knew the people first needed fresh ears to hear it in this new age. They needed preparation, context, and receptivity. They needed to know who they were now (St. Paul's "saints") before they could receive the Word and later be open to it. And it worked! It took a while for them to contextualize the scripture, to learn that they are Church, but it paid off. To this day I'm convinced that, when the time is ripe, every few years, preachers should abandon the homily for a period and, with the sermon, go back and educate, invite, prepare, and renew the focus of the people.

Precious nostalgia: After a few years, I was in the sacristy while some ladies were cleaning in the church. A group of visitors happened to come by (we had many visitors because they'd heard of our vibrant community) and, as they went around the very lovely space, one of the visitors exclaimed out loud, "My, what a beautiful church!" and, without skipping a beat, one of the cleaning ladies replied, "Yes, and the building is nice too!" Inside the sacristy, I gave God the high-five while shouting, "Yesss!" to myself. We had arrived. We were Church.

Today, in light of this book, were I still pastor, I might take some considerable sermon time to hit on two themes. One is the theme of solidarity—so needed in a fractious society and Church. I would redefine and reposition the churchy categories of the Mystical Body of Christ and the Communion of Saints. I know most of the people at church don't know everyone there, but I want to be sure they all understand that we are here as a People of God, as a unit. We share a common baptism, a common christening, a common "Christ-en-ing." We are a collective witness *and* we're united with our spiritual brothers and sisters throughout the world who this day will break open the very word and the very bread we share. I would stress that this is not a place of private pieties but a gathering of the whole Church. We are engaged in liturgy, in *public* worship. In short, in this age of individualism, I would try to raise their consciousness of what it means to be "Catholic," their sense of solidarity, the virtue and the rightness of communal worship, and their defining commitment to the poor.

The second theme, in these days of the shameful lingering effects of the clergy sexual abuse crisis when the bishops have lost all credibility, I would remind them that genuine reform demands official lay oversight and collaboration, and then hit on the theme of mission. I would re-explain and reaffirm their innate baptismal gifts, rights, and their identity as Church alongside of and in tandem with the clergy—and their mutual evangelical co-responsibility (all Vatican II truisms). They do not *participate* in the mission of the bishops as the old chauvinist definition of Catholic Action put it. They *have* the mission in virtue of baptism. This necessitates collaboration. With these identities in place—solidarity and baptismal mandate—with the wider context of the Sunday assembly understood, I would return to the homily.

The Stopwatch Crowd

How did we ever get to the sacrosanct enshrinement of the eight-to-ten-minute homily? I suspect, as we noted previously, that while our Protestant brethren focused on preaching, Catholics focused on celebrating and that may be the difference. Not that they were uniformly sterling preachers. Long windedness sometimes plagues them. Anthony Trollope skewed them in *Barchester Towers*,

> "There is perhaps, no greater hardship at present inflicted on mankind in civilized and free countries than listening to sermons.... No one but a preaching clergyman can revel in platitudes, truisms, and un-truisms and yet receive, as his undisputed privilege, the same respectful demeanor as though words of impassioned eloquence or persuasive logic fell from his lips....No one can rid himself of the preaching clergyman. He is the bore of the age...the nightmare that disturbs our Sunday rest."

For the Catholic clergyman the eight-to-ten-minute homily is forever fixed in the Catholic mind, while the usher's aside, "Make it short, Father" is often the cheery (but slightly menacing) warning. The result is that we preachers feel that if we go too long, the people will hurl missallettes at us or, like the Israelites of old, murmur, murmur, murmur. Pope Francis himself has pleaded, "No more than ten minutes, please!" That makes sense, especially in the light of the parking lot logistics. Preach too long and you back up traffic. Of course, one solution—some parishes really need to consider this—would be to space Masses better so there's plenty of time for the outgoing and incoming congregations to avoid backup. Anyway, windy homilies *are* a bore, so the ten-minute limit works. Still, I sometimes do wonder if we warned the people, why we couldn't extend the homily a bit longer or perhaps have one Mass that is advertised as having, say, a fifteen-15 or even twenty-minute homily for those Catholics who really would like more extended and deeper nourishment. There's got to be a number of them—or are there? Realistically, I suspect the negative votes would be overwhelming. Just a thought.

Pity the Preacher

As for the preacher: He's human too, you know, and has some off days like everyone else. Sometimes he is overextended and overstressed: a funeral on Saturday morning, a wedding in the afternoon, multiple Masses on Sunday perhaps at different churches. Give him some slack. Forgive his occasional bloopers: "At that time, Jesus came from Nazareth into Galilee and was baptized by Jordan in the John." They happen.

An occasional compliment and a word of encouragement would help.

Otherwise, if you're upset with your pastor, try a chain letter. That is, simply send a letter noting such to six other parishes who are tired of their pastors too. Then bundle up your pastor and send him to the church at the bottom of the list. In one week you will receive 1,643 pastors, and one of them should be perfect. Have faith in this letter. One church broke the chain and got their old pastor back in less than three weeks!

Eat or Stare

This is a "fools rush in where angels fear to tread" observation. It concerns what has become an entrenched and a dearly beloved devotion. It is Benediction and Eucharistic Adoration fully promoted by bishops, encouraged by pastors, and loved by devotees. You see why I'm nervous in bringing this up and criticizing it. But hear me out. I point to Vatican II's insistence that the Eucharist is at the heart of the community's faith. The community meal, in which Jesus is present in the Breaking of the Bread and mingling of the wine, carries imperatives of take, break, drink, eat, and share. Do these things when you gather together "in memory of me." The words "in memory of me" imply that we carry the Eucharist with us wherever we go after we leave Mass. The Eucharist is dynamic. But to take the Bread, extract it from the community's presence, from its communal context, from its innate dynamism and put it behind glass to be stared at stagnates the Eucharistic action of the Last Supper. The private passivity of "Kneel and Adore" doesn't do justice to the community's "Take and Eat." It seems we have objectified Jesus and subverted the spiritual energy that impels us to do likewise: break open our lives and share them in the service of others. That's why I whisper that Benediction is a lovely devotion, yet a misguided one.

As for Jesus in the tabernacle, that is a latecomer, too. The preservation of the Eucharist in the early Church, off on the sideline or in the home, was done solely for the means of viaticum, that is, to be hastened to the sick and dying. The practice (often reversed now) of having the tabernacle off to the side or in a nearby alcove testifies to this ancient practice. So, I suggest a replacement. I suggest that the "kneel and adore" mantra is more gloriously fulfilled by the one devotion precisely designed for that purpose: the icon. The icon, by nature, is contemplative art. Created in an attitude of profound mystical prayer and humility, the icon invites us to another world. Instead of the monstrance on the altar that holds Jesus prisoner, I suggest we substitute the icon as the focal point that pulls us into deep mystery and holy Presence. It would take time to make the substitution, but with lots of instruction and considerable courage it could happen.

However, it never will. Just a thought! Societies and ministries devoted to perpetual adoration and round the clock Eucharistic adoration can Google the Vatican to turn me in.

Masses Differ

This passing remark notes what you have always observed, namely, that Masses have their own clientele, personality, atmosphere, and devotees. The Saturday evening Mass is the darling of the pre-dinner, early bird crowd. Mass for them is a stop on the way to the restaurant or weekend play. The first Mass on Sunday morning might catch those needing to leave early and get on the road—the golfers, fishermen, soccer players, Knights of Columbus, or the visit to grandma. Mid-morning is the comfort zone for families, parents, teens, and kids. The last Mass sometimes fills the "last chance" slot. It tends to draw the preoccupied crowd.

As I said, they each offer different personalities, often with different music—traditional or contemporary choir, folk group, or kids' Mass. For this reason, a homily that goes over well at one Mass might fall flat at another. Over the years, the same people tend to attend the same Mass and sit in the same pews (don't dare violate the sacred space!) and a kind of sub-community is formed. If the pew is empty, it causes concern: it must mean that the occupants are travelling or have died. The ushers are old familiar faces. Yes, each Mass has its own tone.

Frustrating Advice

One of my *Arrgh* annoyances is to listen to a preacher urge the people to go apart like Jesus to reconnect with the Center. For that "apart" time, he wisely suggests retreats, days of recollection, daily meditation, and spiritual reading as a beginning—but then, most *un*wisely, most frustratingly, offers no resources! So, I say that, if the preacher is suggesting to the congregation to engage the alternate universe of spiritual reading, he must have a suggested list ready in the bulletin for that Sunday. More than that, there are some wonderful daily reading booklets that take comparatively little time to sit with for a while. There are attractive Catholic websites for adults and young adults, and Catholic magazines that would benefit every household. There are intriguing blogs, bible study groups, podcasts, small faith sharing communities, and so on. All should be shared many times with the congregation in ways they can take home.

The Parish Bulletin

While we're at it, the parish bulletin, paid for by the advertisers, is surely a practical and sensible tool for conveying staff information, phone numbers, hours of services, ministries, and current happenings. But I've always thought it was underused. It could convey much more and even made interesting enough so that people will reach out for it as they leave church—not *enter* it! For example, in the post-Vatican II days, I would find one-page articles, editorials, explanations, and so on from various sources, copy them and insert them into the bulletin each week. (It was our every-Friday- after-Mass-with- coffee-and-donuts-and-lots-of-laughter ministry.) Our survey showed an exceptionally high readership. People read them on the way home and at home and then shared them, which meant that a lot of education went on week after week.

A "Pastor's Corner" is always welcome, but we did encourage parishioners to write short pieces. We listed community events and recommended especially good articles and books. Today we surely would have listed websites and blogs for adults and young people. Rightly anxious parents frequently confide that their college or young adult children are drifting from the church or, often as not, have trouble with some church doctrines. They need direction from the parish suggesting some resources. The bulletin can be a powerful evangelizing tool- and it can be interesting. There's got to be some talented parishioner out there who can turn the bulletin around.

There are two cautions, however. I'm not sure about this, but I think that, like a professor does in a classroom for his or her limited students, you are permitted to reproduce copyrighted articles and editorials for a similarly limited congregation. Check on this. The second caution is more serious. A lot depends on the pastor. If he is either very right-wing conservative or very left-wing liberal, you're libel to get unbalanced, skewed articles that may do more harm than good, or be more divisive than unifying. Nevertheless, the parish bulletin has great potential to be an educating, evangelizing, and dialoging tool.

Parish Hopping

Old loyalties have declined as today people parish shop. Some forty years ago, eighty-five percent of Catholics attended the parish where they lived. Today's surveys show that more than thirty percent of parishioners drive past their parish church to another parish of their choice. What is obvious to all is that, overall, attendance has declined. If some forty-two percent attended in 1985, then today only about twenty-four percent do so. Women, by the way, still predominate, making up sixty-four percent of the congregations.

Blessing from One's Tradition

Apropos of nothing I've written so far, I would like to end with this observation. Among its myriad joys, one of the divisive irritations of Christmas is the annual cultural war over Christmas trees, menorahs, and crèches on public property—and whether to say *Merry Christmas, Holiday Greetings,* or *Happy Holidays.* It's a sad testimony that something as simple as this generates heated antagonisms and court cases, that intolerance and personal offence triumph normal everyday sensible civility.

I offer a suggestion here. *Bless one another from the deepest source of your tradition.* Yes, whether it's 'Happy Kwanza', 'Happy

Ramadam', 'Happy Hanukkah', 'Merry Christmas' or 'Happy Holidays,' draw on the best of your tradition and bless one another from its depths. If the atheists find the word "bless" offensive, they can offer a greeting from the best of their humanist concerns. So, a "Happy Kwanza" from you evokes a "Happy Hanukkah" from me. A "Happy Holidays" from me evokes a "Merry Christmas" or "Seasons Greetings" from you. Despite the libertine fanatics, civilization will not fall if a government employee—say, a postal clerk—says, "Merry Christmas!" and evokes one of these myriad responses from the customer.

The thing is, we've just blessed or wished well to one another from our different places. Like people exchanging native foods with one another, we're exchanging the best of what we value. It's all a take-away from St. Paul, who wrote, "Rejoice in hope…exercise hospitality. Bless those who persecute you, bless and do not curse them... Do not repay anyone evil for evil; be concerned for what is noble in the sight of all" (Romans, 12:12-18). That's it. It's noble. It's generous. It's good will. Something positive has taken place. We have just drawn from our traditions and wished each other well from a source that matters to us. We should be delighted and enlarged by the exchange, not angry and diminished by the specter of political correctness. Maybe you can get a campaign, a national movement, going here. Suggested motto: "It's Holiday Time: Share Your Tradition." Suggested logo: a bridge.

Questions for Discussion

1. What do you think of the notion of the temporary use of the sermon as prelude to and preparation for the homily?
2. What do you think of the two readings preceding the gospel at Mass?
3. Do the readings help give you a fuller sense of the Bible, and a wider sense of the riches of scripture?
4. Do you generally remember the readings? Discuss.

5. Would you like to keep the scripture readings, or would you like to replace them with one non-biblical reading that is understandable to everyone and related to the gospel?
6. Are you content with the ten-minute homily (but not longer)? Why or why not?
7. What do you think of the "Blessing from One's Tradition" campaign?

Pastoral Suggestion

We added two ceremonies to the baptisms celebrated at Mass. First, with some kidding, I would ask, who is the oldest person here? After some bantering, someone raises his or her hand. Then, I would ask that person to approach and silently lay his or her hands on the head of the newly baptized as a visible sign of the passing on of the tradition. No words. It's a quiet, moving, reverent moment, a hushed sign of grace. To see an eighty or ninety-year-old move slowly down the aisle and rest his or her hands on an infant is tableau to remember. Lastly, I would ask the parents to tell the congregation what they wish for their child.

PART III

THE CHALLENGES

Going deeper, this section examines some larger issues related to church going.

13

EMPTY SEMINARIES: WHAT HAPPENS WHEN WE RUN OUT OF PRIESTS?

QUESTION: WHAT HAPPENS WHEN you go to church and there is no priest there? Sometimes churchgoers in certain sections of the country don't feel the absence. That's because usually there's some old retired priest around (like me) to celebrate Mass. However, as my generation passes on, they too will know what many parts of the world know: Masses are celebrated once a month, every six months, once a year, or every several years. The sacraments are not celebrated.

There is a sharp drop in vocations in traditional countries like Poland and Spain. For a concrete example, let's take a quick look at fabled Ireland, "the land of Saints and Scholars," the fully church-going Catholic country who had so many priests that for centuries it sent the excess abroad. Today, in what seems like the blink of an eye, there is almost total collapse. In the 1960s, there were more than 2,000 students for the priesthood in Ireland. Convents, like the local churches, were full. Seminaries abounded. St. Malachy Seminary in Belfast recently closed after 185 years. Today Ireland has only one functioning seminary, Maynooth, and it has, as of now, only *six* seminarians! The average age of today's clergy is 70 and retirees, like those here in America, who hoped to live a leisurely life they so richly deserved, are asked to take on the workload of younger priests. It is, therefore, quite possible that in the foreseeable time some priest in Ireland will be the "last of the Mohicans" and Ireland will have no more priests. Moreover, because of centuries-old density of priests and religious, Ireland never had a need to push the diaconate and so they have comparatively few deacons. The result is sacramental scarcity. There are very few to administer the sacraments. Some bishops have gone so far as to commission laypeople to conduct funerals in the absence of a priest. The usual suspects for the demise: a secular culture, instant communications, more exciting options for the young, the stain and repulsion of the clergy sexual scandal, a restrictive, fossilized out-of-touch Church, the failure of renewal, the mass formation of a materialistic consumerist class, and so on. Whatever, the possibility of a "no priest land" is here.

Our Country

Take a look at our own country. Some stats to get your attention: In 1965 there were almost 36,000 priests in the United States. By 1998, that number had dropped to some 31,000. Today it hovers around 17,500—nearly half that number. Yet, thanks to the Hispanics, as we have seen, the Catholic population has doubled. Between those who have left the priesthood (some 20,000 or more) and the lack of vocations, there is a catastrophic shortage of priests. About 500 priests are ordained each year (only 430 in 2018), but that does not come near to replacing the number of priests who die or those who are inactive due to illness or retirement. To put it another way, today one out of every five parishes in the US is without a priest, as deacons, religious sisters, or laypeople lead them. Some priests are in charge of three, four, or even seven parishes! Talk about a recipe for burnout! It's never easy anyway for two or more parishes to share one priest, and I can tell you it's not easy for the priest himself to serve several parishes. He's a man without a country and that's not good for his emotional or spiritual equilibrium, not good for him to come home to an empty rectory that once housed several curates or assistants. Loneliness is a serious problem. Parishes today routinely subtract Masses. Catholic military chaplains are sorely needed, but there are none to spare. Again, imagine any big corporation dealing with a drastic shortage of its middle management and not sounding the alarm. Yet we don't hear enough of our priest shortage.

Vocations are seriously down all over the world. Seminaries have closed or merged. Life, as we have seen, is so fast, distractions so pervasive, and consumption so standard that many young men never get around to considering the priesthood as their vocation. In former days, when there were few options for middle class or poor boys, these would gravitate to the priesthood. Today there are endless options in an affluent wired world along with the appeal of Silicon Valley's twenty-something millionaires. Then, too, in a world of short-term relationships, a long-term commitment is not that attractive. Nor, to understate the matter, are the young drawn to celibacy.

Finally, the traditionally nearly infallible attraction to garner vocations has degraded or disappeared: the parish priest. The parish priest as friend, model, and effective recruiter no longer exists, not only because his numbers have declined but also because, since the sexual abuse scandals, no priest wants to be alone with a child—and vice versa. Likewise, Catholic parents, who today have fewer children, do not want to "waste" their sons on a less than esteemed vocation; nor these days, smarting from the revelations of sexual abuse there, do parents want to send off a son to a seminary knowing that abusive behavior potentially awaits him. All around, unlike yesteryear, there's no upgrade in being a priest today. There is some flickering of hope because the Hispanic and Vietnamese immigrants are producing a disproportionate number of vocations to the priesthood and religious life, yet hardly in sufficient numbers.

Options

So, badly hurting Church officials are strategizing over several options. There is, of course, the question of a married clergy and its pros and cons, its finances, spousal tensions, the possibility of divorce, a two-tiered priesthood, a devaluation of the genuine charism of celibacy, and so on. At least a married clergy is in our tradition and, therefore, quite possible. I suspect something will be worked out here sooner rather than later as the crisis grows increasingly intolerable—certainly before any consideration of ordaining women since this is not in the tradition, and especially since Pope John Paul II seemingly prohibited it in 1994: "I declare that the Church has no authority whatsoever to confer priestly ordination on women, and that judgment is to be definitively held by all the Church faithful." I say "seemingly" because the issue still surfaces. For example, the severe shortage of a celibate male clergy in the Amazon region of Africa is so profound that in practice women have taken over as parish leaders and ministers as they conduct baptisms, weddings, and bring Communion to other communities. The result is that the Vatican is currently looking into ordaining married men and female deacons. Anyway, celibacy may become optional instead of being across the board. Poll-wise, the laity seem open to this. Besides, celibacy really only works when it is tied to asceticism. The celibate priest who drives the high-end car, lives in a small palace, travels abroad frequently, takes many vacations, has tickets to all the best shows, dines at the best restaurants, savors the best wines, and has front seats at coveted football games is hardly the celibate who has given all for Christ. And he gets to sleep all night.

Then there's the possibility of ordaining those called *viri probati*, "men of proven worth." You know, those solid men you know who are genuine, involved in parish life, and about whom you would say, "He would make a wonderful priest." His marriage is solid, his kids gone, his finances stable, his spirituality sound—all of which would alleviate the pressures of financing him. He would not need to go to a seminary. He would have a similar formation to that of today's married deacon. He would be local, proposed, raised up, so to speak, by the local community. If not retired, he could continue his secular job. He would be valuable if he preserved the Eucharist by celebrating weekend Masses. A possibility.

Then there's the tradition of the "simplex priest," which many Catholics don't know about. This goes way back to when the monks— all laymen, remember—needed to have Mass celebrated. They had the local bishop ordain one of them. That monk's duties ended there. In a similar way, there's the seminarian considered not quite ready for the duties of a full-time priest. Like the monastic celebrant, his superiors would ordain him only on the condition that that's *all* he would do: celebrate Mass. He would live his normal life. No pastoral care, no hearing of confessions, no anointing, and no preaching. Just celebrate Mass. We could certainly do this at our local communities and, thus, preserve the Eucharist. Think: We've always had a part-time clergy called the hyphenated priest: the priest-teacher, the priest-scientist, the priest-doctor and, even for a while, the priest-worker. They ply a totally different non-pastoral trade and come to help parishes on the weekends. Pastoral duties, parish community, and liturgies do not fit into their lives, but they're there when we need Mass celebrated. Then they return to their proper calling. The parish simplex priest could be the priest-plumber. Remember, St. Paul was a tent maker.

Question: Does the oft quoted, "Thou art a priest forever" mean "forever" in the sense that it's your only job *never* to be traded in? Not really. This fact sets us up to consider a time-limited priesthood: the one who is a full-time priest and, while remaining so "forever," at some point changes careers. A young man could sign on for, say, ten years, and at the end, either re-up for another ten or honorably move on to another career. We have that in effect already. Think of the priests who have been legitimately laicized. They are "priests forever," but do not exercise the ministerial priesthood. They are now married and employed elsewhere, even while always remaining a priest. Speaking of that, what *about* those priests who have left and married and are still faithful Catholics? Shouldn't they be re-tapped?

And yet, having expounded these options in our time of crisis, in no way do I wish to eliminate the charism and countercultural sign of celibacy so needed in a permissive society. In a similar way, the monasteries that needed Mass celebrated and ordained one of their monks for the task, had no desire to denigrate or replace the celibate priesthood. As the debate over women's ordination goes on, I would opt meanwhile for a revival of female religious orders and diaconate and then seek for the hierarchy to integrate women more fully into the actual governance of the church.

Finally, since we're discussing priests and since the issue has come up here and there as a major roadblock to renewal, let's add a word about clericalism. Clericalism may be defined as the caste system that elevates the ordained Catholic male priesthood onto a pedestal high above the ordinary people and downgrades those not of this caste to a lower status. It produces a hermetically sealed clerical elite who are often unaware of, if not indifferent to, the needs and aspirations of the laity and harbor a superiority over women. Transparency is in short supply. Such a closed system lives apart, celebrates apart and makes rules apart, often insensitive to the realities of life. Clericalism, in other words, refers to that out-of-touch clergy club of celibate males whose minds, hearts, and lifestyles are in privileged aristocratic mode. All this is no way disparages those many priests who have served the people in great humility and heroism. It's just to say that such clericalism, strongly scolded by Popes Benedict XVI and Francis, has and does exist. It creates a divide of sympathies, loyalties, and pastoral sensitivities—and a-mindset that has spawned the most serious crisis in the Catholic Church since the Protestant Reformation. To this, we now turn.

The Elephant in the Sanctuary

It is, alas, a sign of the times that, even in a light-hearted book such as this, I cannot fail in a chapter on priests to expound a bit on the never-ending clergy sexual scandal alluded to in this chapter. Beneath the searing lurid revelations lies the intractable and almost universal fact of cover up by bishops. *That's* the core of the problem. They knew full well the facts, shamefully moved errant perpetrators around and hid the evidence in a vault. As I read the reports of abuse, I was consistently struck by any lack of visceral disgust and horror on the part of bishops and officials. Responses were bureaucratic. They protected the institution and put it first. There's no getting around their pivotal complicity and guilt. The conclusion is obvious: of all the cacophony of ecclesiastical and secular suggestions to address the problem of clerical sexual abuse the most critical element is episcopal leadership or lack thereof. That means there is clearly and urgently the need to reform the way bishops are chosen.

The blunt fact is that the current system relies on cronyism. Too often the criteria for appointment rests solely on one's orthodoxy and on whether the episcopal candidate has made any negative public announcements on celibacy, married priests, or contraception.

Either they have matriculated from Rome or had a cardinal patron accelerate the process, and that's why we sometimes receive bishops straight from administration with little or no pastoral experience. Connections and administrative gifts matter, but not pastoral gifts. And it's all done in secret.

My two cents to reform this process: First, I would suggest that all episcopal candidates must have spent *at least* ten years in parish work and not just as weekend help. They must have experienced the people firsthand. Secondly, ask the people to assess the candidate's pastoral sensitivity and effectiveness, compassionate ministry and the absence of careerism—all virtues that, according to then-Cardinal Ratzinger, are qualities as important for a bishop as his orthodoxy. Thirdly, like the old threefold publication of banns of marriage for engaged couples, every diocesan paper throughout the land should be required to publish the name of the one being considered for the office of bishop and list his name online. This might prevent any embarrassing revelations later on.

None of this is novel by the way. It belongs to the long tradition enshrined in the second-century *Apostolic Tradition of Hippolytus*, which flatly declared, "Let him be ordained as bishop who has been chosen by all the people." This sentiment was echoed by Pope St. Celestine in the fifth century, who said, "Let a bishop not be imposed upon the people whom they do not want," and his successor, Pope St. Leo, who declared, "He who has to preside over all must be elected by all. Let a person not be ordained against the wishes of the Christians and whom they have not explicitly asked for." Most people are not aware of this ancient tradition. They must reclaim it.

The laity needs to be officially involved in matters of the Church, a fact that I shall emphasize in chapter 16. One of the quiet revolutions for renewal, as I shall mention there, is a new rebalance in the future Church: the decline and death of clericalism and the rise of baptismal awareness of the gifts of the laity. A new alignment is waiting to be born and you want to be a part of it.

Well, this is a lot to think about. But, remember, the people have a right to the Eucharist. If you can see to it that you get to church, the bishops should see to it that you have an authorized celebrant waiting for you when you get there and one who is pastorally and ethically sound. So, speak up. Fill out the surveys. The priest short-age would be a good topic for discussion at the next parish council, altar rosary, and men's guild meetings!

Discussion Questions

1. What do you think of a married clergy?
2. What do you think of those married priests who were canonically laicized returning to celebrate Mass?
3. What do you think of ordaining chosen married men from the parish to take care of weekend Masses?
4. What do you think of restoring the "simplex" priest?
5. What do you think of women priests?
6. Some have asked why would women want to join a priesthood they call "a cozy clerical elite"? Would adding woman cure it? What do you think?
7. What will happen when the last priest dies?

Pastoral Suggestion

Even some forty years ago, it was clear that the pool of priests was dwindling. So, I told the people that to prepare for the future they would have to learn of an alternate liturgy. There are three official ones: the Mass, the Sacraments, and the Divine Office. Would they like to try the communal Divine Office? Yes; so they choose the Thursday morning prayer hour with its opening hymn, opening prayer, chanting of psalm 42, scripture reading, a reflection, the intercessions or prayers of the faithful, the Our Father, Communion (we added this), and a closing prayer and hymn. It would take the same length of time as the Mass.

I took a month or two to teach them the origin, background, the meaning, and rich-ness of the Divine Office. I brought in a professional to teach them how to chant, and then we began. We dropped Mass on Thursday morning and in its place chanted the Divine Office. For about four months I led the Office till they got used to it, and then I did my famous *Glenmary Dance* that has always been an integral part of my ministry.

The term *Glenmary Dance* comes from the Glenmary Fathers, who move into no-priest territories, recruit natives, establish parishes, and then move on. Their job is done. The principle is when the student learns then the teacher moves on and lets the student own the project. When the lay people began to lead the Divine Office, I moved to the front pew, then gradually the middle pew, then the last pew, and then finally I danced out the door. It was theirs. I had done my *Glenmary Dance*. We wound up with Mass four mornings a week with the Divine Office on Thursdays. (We never had a Saturday morning Mass because of a possible funeral, frequently a wedding, plus confessions, and the evening vigil Mass. It was all too much when you're alone.)

Let me take time to recount the blessings of this move. First, the people loved it and learned to appreciate the richness of the Divine Office. Secondly, lay people became quite adept at taking turns leading the liturgy, expounding the scripture and sharing reflections. In fact, on occasion, when a priest didn't show up for Sunday Mass and I was away, people simply got up from the pews and took over and led a scripture, gave a reflection, led prayer, distributed Communion, and then led the closing hymn. It seems to me, in today's crisis, every parish should routinely establish this practice.

On a personal note, as usual, the people humbled me almost to tears. As I sat among them as a participant and listened to their profound reflections honed from trying to live a Christ-like life in today's climate and raise children with a million commercial Herods trying to take their souls, I marveled at their holiness and prayer life. I realized how privileged, predictable, and safe my own life was. These were the saints whose shoes I wasn't worthy to tie.

Thirdly, so captivating did the Divine Office become that in addition, first the men and then later the women, decided to meet at 6:30 a.m. one day each week in our spiritual center chapel to chant it. It was a challenge in the winter! For those who didn't have to run off to work, camaraderie and coffee came afterwards. By the way, at first the men did it and then later the women joined them, but soon the group segregated. As one of the men good-naturedly put it, like the men, the women also arrived in silence—until the next woman arrived! They were simply on different rhythms and preferred different days. Chanting the Divine Office and sharing scripture and reflection at 6:30 a.m. became so popular that still today, some forty years later, it persists. Could this be a good venture for your parish?

14

EMPTY PEWS: WHERE ARE ALL THE OLD PEOPLE?

LET'S BEGIN WITH AN eye-catching statistic: In the 1950s, ninety-five percent of Quebec's population attended Mass. Today only five percent do. Try to take that in. And this free-fall is true all over the world. Catholicism is severely declining in its traditional bastions of support: Europe, South America, the Islands—and here in the United States. When I was ordained in 1955, seventy-five percent of Catholics attended church. A Gallup poll released in May of 2017 shows that church attendance has fallen to thirty-nine percent. Parishes are either closing or blending. The Diocese of Pittsburgh, for example, has announced that it will reduce their 188 parishes to only 57 by 2023. The Archdiocese of Hartford's 212 parishes will be consolidated into eighty-five. The Archdiocese of Chicago likewise plans to consolidate its 351 parishes. The same goes everywhere. The Northeast and Rust Belt have lost thousands of Catholics, while dioceses in the Sun Belt are expanding. As we have noted, the number of clergy has fallen below crisis level and the real possibility of the disappearance of a celibate clergy looms. Diversity is the rule as one in four parishes today offer weekend liturgies in more than one language. An estimated 40,000 lay ecclesial ministers and about 18,000 permanent deacons serve in a variety of roles trying to make it work. New models of parish leadership are struggling to be born.

There are many complicated causes for Catholic defections, or for dropping out of Mass. We can only mention some of the more obvious ones. Once more, the clergy sexual abuse scandal has surely rocked the Catholic world and severely undermined the Church's status as a moral arbiter and guide. The scandal broke in the United States, costing the Church here billions of dollars and forcing several dioceses into bankruptcy. Soon the Church in other countries, encouraged by the publicity and the women's #MeToo Movement, came under fire. So far, there are Ireland, Australia, and Chile where Cardinals and Archbishops have been publicly sued or forced to resign. Nor have we seen the last of it as the crisis has yet to arrive in such Catholic countries as Poland, the Philippines, and Italy. The Church in many parts of the world has indeed turned a corner in child protection, but much remains to be done. The bad odor remains.

Perhaps an even larger impact on loyal Catholics is that society has veered in a sharp liberal and secular direction, seducing the missing youth and adding to the pressures on those who do want to live a faithful spiritual life. In other words, making Mass Matter is enormously hard in a predominate culture that in so many ways implies that Mass *doesn't* matter. In fact, religion itself is really the enemy. Science rules and faith muddies the waters. Biologist Richard Dawkins has pontificated that "not only is science corrosive to religion, religion is corrosive to science." The best-selling author, Steven Pinker of Harvard, one of the world's most influential intellectuals, set the standard for Harvard and other universities when he famously wrote that there is no place for faith in a university curriculum which prizes reason. Distain is right there in our educational system. (I can't help but think of G.K. Chesterton's remark that "a madman isn't one who has lost his reason. A madman is one who has lost everything *but* his reason.") Public schools from grade schools through universities display court-enjoined indifference, if not hostility, to religion to the extent that some students relate that they feel pressured to hide their religiosity. The popular so-called "new atheists" have painted religion as violent, irrational, and even dangerous to the extent it must be exterminated. All the major dominating institutions are far left secular: education, the media, Silicon Valley, global firms, and corporate America. They supply the logos, slogans, news stories, movies, sitcoms, publicity, venues, and celebrities that promote values often at odds with the Church. The point is that consumerist secularism is a cultural saturation thing and trying to escape it is like trying to escape polluted air. There's nowhere to hide.

The Acceptable and Approved Standards

A quick glance at the problem. The sexual revolution of the sixties has triumphed. Living together has gone mainstream and no longer provokes any comment nor does having children out of wedlock. They're part of the accepted culture. In fact, statistically, according to the latest census, more people have children outside of rather than *in* marriage. Same sex marriage is legal in most of the West, from Catholic Ireland to the United States. Abortion on demand is virtually the global norm. Recently, as part of their platform, Democrats have proposed a Reproductive Health Act that would not require doctors to care for a baby who survives abortion. The newborn would simply be allowed to die. Abortions would be legal up to the moment of birth. There are already calls in Britain and Europe to exclude from the medical professions persons who are unwilling to perform abortions or promote them. Countries like Canada have made abortion such a fundamental human right that it will deny federal funding to any group that opposes it. Ideological uniformity is now imposed and policed by the state.

Today there are fewer Down Syndrome babies born as they are routinely aborted. Euthanasia is now legal in most countries including Australia, Italy, and Ireland. Among the United States, Hawaii has recently joined Washington, DC, the state of Washington, Oregon, California, Vermont, and Colorado in legalizing assisted suicide. Among the public, approval of assisted suicide has risen from thirty-seven percent in 1947 to seventy percent since 1990. A new factor behind these statistics is the demographic reality that the elderly will outnumber babies in ten years. These are the baby boomers who saw their parents experience horrible deaths and want to avoid similar ends. Human eggs are sold on eBay. In Brazil, wealthy single women and lesbian couples are driving a surging market for North American sperm, with a heavy tilt towards the gene packets that produce white-skinned blue-eyed babies. [12] Soon, you will see Brazilian children named Pedro Rodrigues looking for all the world like Paddy Murphy. Polygamy and infanticide are in the wings.

Then there are the outright overt anti-religions, anti-Catholic prejudices. For example, there are those who want churches to be listed as places of "public accommodation" so they can be open to state and federal regulations. One state had even proposed that churches welcoming non- parishioners to a spaghetti dinner or letting them use the church for a wedding would be sufficient to subject them to rules about transgender bathrooms! This harkens back to the time some 90 years ago when the anti-Catholic Scottish Rite Masons, supported by the Klu Klux Klan, tried to pass a law forcing all children to attend the public schools. Most states have some form of prohibition of public dollars going to religious institutions. In recent memory, the courts have forced Catholic Charities in Boston, San Francisco, and Illinois to shut down their adoption services because they would not place children with same sex couples (the children are very much the losers.) In my area, the ACLU recently sued an animal shelter because a priest gave the blessing of the animals there on the feast of St. Francis!

The Daily Seductions

Then there are the everyday secularizations of the accepted culture that slowly sap our spirit. The Sunday rest has become the Sunday frenzy of shopping and soccer. Beginning in early September, the full barrage of Christmas-inspired consumerism unleashes. Black Friday, followed by Cyber Monday followed by pre-, current-, and post-Christmas sales are the norm. Many homes, pre-Advent, are already decorated with lots of high-tech lights. Immediately after Christmas, we brace for New Year's Eve, Valentine's Day, St. Patrick's Day, followed by pre- and post-Easter sales and Amazon Prime Day. It's all relentless speed. There is no time to savor life anymore, no time to go beneath the surface since surface-to surface keeps calling to us. The next distraction is always around the corner. We're all caught up in a vast, attractive consumerism.

Well, I could go on and on, but you get the point. The fact is, as we said, the cultural atmosphere is intractably consumerist, secular, and fast—quite hostile to the interior life, the religious life, especially since religion has been prohibited from the public square and left pretty much on its own without any societal support. Catholics, in particular, feel the burden of such homogenized secularization. Parents are rightly concerned over such an uphill fight to pass on the faith because in this climate it's almost impossible not to be seduced.

All these things help explain why Mass attendance has dropped. The challenge to us means that we must be more "intentional" Christians. We all need to work hard to maintain the faith and understand why Mass Matters. Christianity doesn't have to rise or fall by becoming the religion of the state or an entirely private affair. Publicly showing up on Sunday, joining faith sharing groups, breaking open the Word, breaking Bread and witnessing the rest of the week is the tried and true formula for spiritual renewal. Just as early Christianity spawned great apologists for the faith, we must become more religiously literate by moving beyond the mass consumerist books, magazines, and media in general. We must become more evangelical by witnessing to our faith. Today, there is a plethora of Catholic resources and programs in which to tap into. Invest in them.

Discussion Questions

1. What do you think, withdraw from secular society or confront it?
2. What do you find most challenging in trying to hold onto the faith? What bothers you?
3. What practices do you find helpful for nourishing your faith?
4. Where and how do you see hope?
5. Do you regularly read books or magazines of faith? Which ones?

Pastoral Suggestions

You can't always rely on a tone-deaf press to give you the straight news on religion. That's why it's so necessary to visit reliable sources and subscribe to some good Catholic magazines and digital platforms. Among the latter are suggested:

CRUX is a general site that covers carefully and honestly all things of interest to the Catholic Church. It will give you more accurate information than the general media—a kind of must-have digital daily newsletter every informed Catholic must have. Just visit the *Crux* website and you'll get directions on how to subscribe. I use it all the time.

Then there are three very neat and charming blogs: *Whispers in the Loggia*, *Busted Halo*, and *ReasonableCatholicism.com*. Finally, there is the website www.CredibleCatholic.com. It has various PowerPoint components or modules that talk about aspects of the faith. It takes on questions raised by ordinary Catholics and skeptics alike. It's a website for everyone, from the older people to younger Catholics and also for students seeking answers. It's like an electronic catechism. Try it.

15

EMPTY FUTURE: WHERE ARE ALL THE YOUNG PEOPLE?

WHATEVER THE ANSWER TO this chapter's title question is, one thing we know for sure is that they are not in church. All over the country, parents are grieving over their adult children who no longer go to church, who do not have their children baptized, and who even declare that they are atheists. Their children remain decent, moral, and even engage in works of justice and charity—but no church anymore. Spirituality, *si*! Church, *non*!

The statistics are well known, the causes complex. Except for Islam that, due to immigration and high birth rates, is rapidly increasing globally, every other religion has decreased, especially Christianity with Catholics by far suffering the most losses of all. In 2016, for example, there were more than 30 million people who referred to themselves as "former Catholics." "I was raised Catholic, but…" or "I am a recovering Catholic…" are all too frequent comments today. That's a big loss. Imagine some corporation losing those numbers! Some say there are more ex-Catholics than present ones. [13]

And the youth? Bad news. Surveys show that among those Catholics who choose to leave the Church, seventy-four percent do so between the ages of ten and twenty, while an eighty-seven percent say it is for good. Nearly two-thirds identify as no longer Catholic by age seventeen. One national study found that the millennials (those born between the 1980s and early 2000s) "are the least religious generation of the last six decades and possibly in the nation's history." Some are hostile. One YouTuber got more than 30 million views for his video, "Why I Hate Religion, But Love Jesus." As we said, it's tough on parents. One woman who remains a practicing Catholic bemoans that her sixteen-year-old son claims to be an atheist and her twelve-year-old daughter is an agnostic. Only a deeply secular and unsettled culture could produce this all too common scenario.

To put it as simply as possible, today's youth do not have the experience of growing up Catholic. They have been and are being raised in a highly secularized society where faith is seen as one option among many. The widespread alienation of the young from organized religion is due not so much to some personal inner spiritual defect as much as the general, across the board, modern way of life that they have inherited: the climate of skepticism, distrust, disbelief and the broken institutions that used to support society. They ask, "Where can I go for truth and hope?" They respond, "Not to a church that harbors predators, rejects gays, and downgrades women. Not to a government that lies, is broken, dysfunctional, and divided. Not to the media that purveys fake news and the fake people ("bots") who create it. Not to schools that block free speech and teach them one-dimensional liberalism. Not to the politicians who line their own pockets and serve Big Business." Only the military gets some grudging respect. By default, the only reliable place left, the young say, is their own thoughts and own individual decisions. On top of this, they also have to deal with poor job prospects, student debt, anxiety, drug and alcohol abuse and, for too many, broken homes.

The Camps

The Center for Applied Research in the Apostolate (CARA) classifies the alienated youth into three general camps: the injured, the drifters, and the dissenters. The injured have had bad experiences with their families: divorce, illness, death, non-practice (non-practicing parents exercise a big negative influence). Understandably, for those who have been sexually abused by clergy it will only be an unusual one who finds their way back. The drifters just find the Church and its rules and rituals meaningless, not part of the real world, while the dissenters are just that: dissenting from the Church's teaching on sex, contraception, gay marriage, abortion, and on general teachings that don't make sense to them like salvation, heaven, hell and, as always for everyone, the question of how a good and merciful God can allow so much suffering.

Anyway, most young people just don't drop Catholicism or religion entirely. They might go to Mass with the family on Christmas or Easter. Some join other denominations. Most simply eschew a specific religion while remaining spiritual. As mentioned, for those who came from broken or non-practicing families, there are, unfortunately, no inner tapes, sights, sounds, no memories to surface later that might call them back, and so any road back will be a difficult one and, most likely, an untraveled one. Any pastor will tell you that Confirmation was Graduation Day for many of these kids. One survey indicates that less than six percent of those confirmed during the week will be present at the following Sunday Mass. And I hate to tell you this, but "They will come back when they have kids of their own" is more wishful thinking than fact. If they do get married (and more are forgoing marriage altogether), it's often not in the Catholic Church. According to Vatican statistics, worldwide there were some 326,079 marriages in the Church in 1990. In 2017, the number fell to just 145,916!

The young, it seems, no longer expect anything *from* the church and have no connection *to* it. That makes it almost impossible to evangelize them. The Church is simply not a part of their lives and we have to accept this truth and work from it. They go through life without ever meeting a priest or pastoral worker. They're interested in the environment, poverty, peace issues but with no necessary reference to the church.

Other Issues

There are other issues that disturb them. Let me list some predominant ones here.

They complain that their needs are not being met. Pious talks about Marian apparitions don't speak to where they are. Some have memories of their parish as that of a service station with little or no community. If they do stray into church among the gray heads, they feel there's no sense of welcome. One twenty-four-year-old relates, "I have spent plenty of time parish shopping. It took me a while to find a sacramental home. I have been the youngest person in the pews many times. I can no longer count the number of churches I have walked in and out of without anyone saying hello and asking what my name was, or if I were new." (Could that be your parish?) Bad homilies, unprepared and boring homilies, or retrograde homilies that "sold" fifty years ago totally turn them off.

Then there's the Church's over-emphasis on Orthodoxy—even to the point of torture and death in some centuries—and little attention to Orthopraxis, the way Catholic people live. They find this hypocritical. "The church is full of hypocrites" is one of their favorite cries. The famous scene from *The Godfather* where Michael Corleone is having his son baptized at the same moment when, on his orders, his henchmen are murdering his enemies comes to mind. The young (and old) know that the Corleones would instantly be called on the carpet for denying the Trinity, but never reprimanded for murder, prostitution, gambling, and corruption. In fact, as for many adults, the lives of some Catholics scandalize them.

The clericalism we wrote of doesn't sit well with them either. As Pope Francis commented, "The community needs a father, a brother, and what they find is a doctor, a professor...a prince." The high-handedness of some bishops and priests, the second-rate status of the laity, and the taken-for-granted perks that ordinary people don't enjoy jar their sense of equality. The young complain that Christianity is more about organized religion than about loving God. Of course, for them, it is axiomatic that religion and science are incompatible. That "truth" has been drummed into their heads at school and so presents a deep tension forcing them, they think, to choose. In summary, they view Christianity as anti-gay, judgmental, and hypocritical.

Seeds of Hope

We must not despair. There are seedlings of hope. While we bemoan the loss of some of the young, others really are on fire for God, especially those who have had the good fortune to be a part of parish youth groups and faith groups at college. If we could harness them, we would have a "great awakening." Remember that the first World Youth Days inaugurated by Pope John Paul II in 1983 attracted millions of young people from around the globe. The charismatic gathering of youth at the Franciscan University of Steubenville attracts more than 50,000 Catholic teenagers each year. Today they gather at similar international, national, and local rallies. There are untold youth groups who rally for Jesus.

You should know that some creative youth outreaches have sprouted around the country. For example, "Theology on Tap", a Chicago based organization, draws thousands of young people to discuss religion over drinks and appetizers. There are many Blogs and websites, like "The Jesuit Post" and "The Alpha Experience" and FOCUS, the latter a peer ministry of The Fellowship of Catholic University Students, and many other organizations who evangelize them where they are.

Thankfully, besides the growing blogs and websites which cater to them, there are signs the hierarchy is now at last getting serious about these young adults. The bishops are reexamining the Church's relationship to youth. They acknowledge that too few dioceses have a director of youth ministry and there is a sense that this must be corrected. They realize that youth and young adult ministries must become a high priority, especially, as we have seen, as America moves towards a Majority Hispanic population.

At this writing in 2018, Pope Francis has announced a general assembly of the Synod of Bishops concerning the youth. Young people between ages sixteen and twenty-nine have been invited to participate in an online survey. The bishops are seriously asking for input and this in itself is a step forward. In short, although there's still a long way to go, there are signs of a belated yet new process of evangelization geared to this most precious group. So far, preliminary in-person meetings with the young people reveal a truly deep and desperate need for guidance in their fragmented and frightening world. They are seeking depth in a shallow society that celebrates the surface. They *are* looking for a platform to engage with religion. They are looking for role models in the faith.

There is a longing. They just don't know how to connect. So far, neither do we.

Church, No; Spirituality, Yes

If at present the motto is "Church *non* and Spirituality *si!*" then we can hope and pray that, for the injured, the drifters, and the dissenters, one day it won't be "either-or" but "both-and." Meanwhile, that phrase deserves some commentary you need to consider. "Spirituality yes, church no." What do these words mean? Spirituality is such a slippery word. Outside of the long traditions and practices of organized religion, its meaning is all over the lot. Outside of Christian spirituality as a way of living one's life in openness to the Spirit around the practices of prayer and gospel values, much of self-styled spirituality seems self-indulgent, invented, private, and cut off from religion's larger wisdom and experience. As scholar Sandra Schneiders sums it up, such self-constructed spirituality "is usually a privatized, idiosyncratic, personally satisfying stance and practice which makes no doctrinal claims, imposes no moral authority outside one's own conscience, creates no necessary personal relationships or social responsibilities, and can be changed or abandoned whenever it seems not to work for the practitioners."[14] A good summary.

It's easy to see, however that such spirituality fits in with our consumerist culture where people construct their own identities. People appropriate the old images and language, disconnecting them from the communal contexts and traditions which gave them meaning in the first place. Without communal support, however, spirituality becomes "my" thing, leaving the practitioner to make up his or her own mind or move on if they feel like it. The nice part (to them) is that this makes them free from the influence of cultural constraints, external authority, and social roles of any kind. Furthermore, fortified with the allergenic word "judgmental" and the school-taught "you-have-your-truth-and-I-have-my-truth," such spirituality insulates them from wider dialogue and discourse. It also immunizes them from any demands because, in their world, external demands do not exist, only options.

But Jesus said, "Not everyone who says to me, "Lord, Lord, will enter the kingdom of heaven but only those who do the will of my heavenly Father" (Matthew 7:21), meaning, yes, there *is* another source of right and wrong beyond my opinion. When in the famous judgment scene in Matthew 25 Jesus, declared in no uncertain terms that, regardless of their opinion, those who did *not* feed, clothe, and visit the least of his sick and imprisoned brothers and sisters will be cast into hell fire, he clearly left us outside measurements by which to live.

The point is, someone else is in play beyond "my" spirituality. There *is* the One who will come "to judge the living and the dead." In short, a self-concocted private spirituality unmoored from communal religion won't do.

As T.S. Eliot put it:

> Why should [people] love the church?
> Why should they love her laws?
> She tells them of life and death
> and all they would forget.
> She is tender where they would be hard
> and hard where they would like to be soft.
> She tells them of evil and sin
> and other unpleasant facts.[15]

Discussion Questions

1. What can parents do to get their children to church?

Pastoral Suggestions

For your married children: Without pushing it too hard, quietly evangelize the grandkids. You have a privileged position. Introduce them to their heritage gently and comfortably. Outside of an outright prohibition from their parents, most grown children have no objection to *their* parents taking the children to church with them when they go. For birthdays or Christmas presents include a Children's Bible. Answer their questions. Above all, tell the stories. Be their example.

Secondly, for your college kids, ask your parish to do the following (make it a new ministry.) In the parish bulletin, let there be a form to fill out giving the name of your son/daughter and their new college address and turn it in to the parish office. With this information, every once in a while, the parish will send the kids a brown envelope potpourri. Include the parish bulletin, a timely excerpt from a magazine, some reflection about the things that bother them, community news, and where to connect with their friends who went to other colleges. Add some books worth reading and, especially for these savvy kids, some terrific peer developed blogs about religion and formats where college kids talk to college kids. Perhaps they will toss the envelope away like some unwanted advertisement, or perhaps not. But it *is* something from home and the people they know. It tells them that their faith community hasn't forgotten them, and that they are still part of something larger.

Specifically for Young Adults

The problem for today's parents is that their kids are growing up in a world unlike anything they grew up in and they don't have answers to their arguments. Their children are products of their age—which means they are immersed in the media and consumerist culture. Parents can at least meet them where they are by giving them on special occasions (birthdays, graduation, Christmas gifts, and so on) "an offer they can't refuse." Such as:

Give them books and blogs. Why not? That's their life's blood. The only thing is that they never, ever check those that might offer them another side to the secular creed they are fed. So, give them an alternative: nothing preachy, pious, or full of platitudes but instead some nifty, smart stuff to which they can relate. So, take note of these winners:

As for books, *Tattoos on the Heart* is the first and, if necessary, only book you want to give your young adult who has fled religion. *Tattoos on the Heart* by Gregory Boyle, S.J. (Free Press) is a fantastic, jaw-dropping story of this Jesuit priest who deals everyday with the drugged, tattooed, often homeless, routinely imprisoned down-and-outs in Los Angeles, the gang capital of the world. Funny, heart-breaking, and fascinating, it will grab your son or daughter immediately. They will love it.

Barking to the Choir. Father Boyle's long-awaited sequel and just as good. Get it. (Read both yourselves. You'll be inspired).

Then, in general, there are books like *Help My Unbelief* and *The WOW Factor*, (Orbis Press) both by William J. O'Malley, S.J. who has taught skeptical students all his life. These books will appeal very much to older adults, as well.

A great book for the faith vs science crowd is by a couple of savvy Jesuits who are scientists working at the famed Vatican Observatory. Delightful, charming, and smart, the book is *Would You Baptize an Extraterrestrial?* by Guy Consolmagno and Paul Mueller (Image Press).

Then there's *Unapologetic: Why, Despite Everything, Christianity Can Still Make Surprising Sense* (London: Faber & Faber, 2012) by Francis Spufford. Funny, sometimes vulgar, and spicy—and your kids will love it.

Now, if you have a very bright, inquiring young adult, you cannot do better than to give him or her the following book. It's *Why Believe?* by John Cottingham (Continuum International Publishing Group). The book is entirely engaging and compelling. It's sharp, appealing and superior in every way. It's a good antidote to the books of the best-selling atheists. Buy it also for your secularist friends. Read it yourself if you have doubts, or just want a good read. After that, move on to Cottingham's *How to Believe*.

Then there are always the great standards, C.S. Lewis' *Mere Christianity* and *The Screwtape Letters*. They will love this second one (it's about a devil and his bumbling apprentice tempter.)

Next, we turn to some selected Blogs & Websites they will find irresistible. Here are some:

The Jesuit Post
www.thejesuitpost.org

This website was designed by the clever Jesuits and is especially for seekers in their 20s and 30s. It's a great source they will love and can easily get hooked on. A fabulous gift.

Alpha Experience
www.facebook.com/catholicconversation

This is another great website designed to appeal to the young (and old.)

Formed
Formed.org

This is another website for youth and young adults.. You can get it free through your parish. Login to formed.org.register, and if you enter your parish's access code (they will give it to you) you can enter your email address and then create your own password. Its content is in Spanish as well as English, and it covers all things Catholic. If your parish is not part of it, you can still do it on your own.

Check out also: "The Edmundite Show" on YouTube.

Finally, you should know—and pass it on to the kids—there are many popular young adult gatherings like the Chicago-founded "Theology on Tap" that bring in speakers, offer drinks and appetizers, and draw in young adults. For example, some six-hundres young people met recently in Milwaukee. Likewise, numerous scripture study programs for young adults are available.

For your teens here are some blog suggestions:

https://lifeteen.com

https://churchpop.com

https://www.catholicteenbooks.com

https://dynamiccatholic.com

https://ascensionpress.com

If you have trouble giving these as gifts, just ask any ten-year-old and they'll help you.

16

A NEW ALLIANCE

WITHOUT STRAYING TOO FAR off course, I think I should end this book with a short caveat. Sometimes, in the justifiable criticism of clericalism and the institutional Church, we may get the impression that we don't need priests or the hierarchy. Nothing could be further from the truth. People of good will (and a sense of history) are seeking reform not rejection. They are seeking balance. They are seeking, especially in the light of the awful clergy sexual abuse crisis, an officially recognized place at the ecclesiastical table where they can have input and demand accountability and oversight. Lay people do not want power—they saw where that led—but partnership.

What we're witnessing today, then, is that new grassroots structures are struggling to emerge alongside of and within the parish churches and within the institutional Church. One thinks of the explosion of bible study groups led by laypeople, contemplation groups, the democratizing of spiritual direction, Catholic Worker houses, the De Colores ministry, the Focolare movement, L'Arche, Taize, St. Egidio's community, and a host of other ministries that are often largely the inspirations of the laity who are in communion with the clergy, though not dependent on the clergy—the old "shared and collaborative ministry" principle in action. What is important right now is not where we were but where we can be, that many voices for change are merging and coalescing, that prophetic voices are speaking out and seeking their places *within* the institution called the Church and not outside it.

We just need to be wary of those who want reform without institutions. It won't work and never has. A society without institutions is simply rootless, chaotic, and lacks memory. Institutions are valuable because they codify and preserve the initial epiphany, the initial experience, and keep it alive. They are repositories of tradition and record, along with the heroes and heroines who preserve both.

The institution we call the Church preserves the revelation, along with the saints and the prophets who embody it. It offers support, symbols, rituals, holy places, nurture, theologies, and leaders. The fact is, we need hierarchy in every phase of life and erasing every authority figure is self-destructive, as history has shown. We see this in the modern heady hope that a free-wheeling, uninhibited Internet would allow everyone to speak freely and exchange ideas. Then the world would be a better place. Wrong. Instead we got polarization, fake news, lies, hackers, and foreign interference in our elections. Facebook has come under fire for letting users raid their data to invade the privacy of its customers. Now we're desperately looking for a referee, a hierarchy, to sort it all out. Think five centuries ago when the Reformation was supposed to spawn "the priesthood of all believers" and instead we got 130 years of violent disagreement and conflict that ended with the restoration of a hierarchy in Church and politics. Two centuries later, the Enlightenment challenged established authority with the promise of full liberty, but we wound up with a reign of terror for those who didn't see it that way and eventually we had to call in a collective hierarchy of world leaders to produce treaties and some order (the League of Nations, United Nations). There are those, in other words, who want an orchestra without a conductor, never appreciating that the music will soon become chaotic and eventually they'll have to send out for one.

So, as we have been saying, the problem is not the hierarchy per se, but the hierarchy and its departments that have grown out of touch and now define themselves by power, privilege, and entitlement, devolving into self-serving entities organically apart from the people they serve. It gets worse when its hand-me-down clericalism tends to treat the laity as children and holiness becomes a two-tiered model with bias toward the clergy and religious. Say "Church," think "hierarchy" covers the deformity.

Even so, we don't want the institution to disappear. We want it reformed because religion, without the boundaries of tradition and institution, has the tendency to dissolve into that old bromide, "It doesn't matter what you believe as long as you're sincere." Lord knows we have enough of that today. Even though we may be exasperated with the way institutional religion sometimes works and will go around seeking a more "pure" church, we should be wary. Father Andrew Greeley, who was always ahead of his time, tells us why:

> "The idea of a pneumatic Church is an attractive one and always has been. A handful of dedicated Christians working in a community in almost invisible fashion, exuding good will and love, and unconcerned about mundane things such as finance, administration, and communication, sounds terribly appealing. But even if it were possible for a community of humans to exist without a formal structure, and it is quite impossible, those who would object to a structured Church and would prefer a pneumatic one should take the matter up with the Founder who wanted his Church to be a thoroughly human organization and seemed prepared to accept the fact that in this human organization there would be all kinds of human imperfections.... The trouble with angry, alienated revolutionaries is that they can't win, they really don't want to win. They are what Irving Howe calls the kamikaze radicals who desire to pull down and destroy so that a fresh new start can be made. But they ignore the lessons of history that real growth is always organic, and that true progress usually comes from reforms of existing structures rather than from the creation of brand new ones." [16]

Then there's Kenneth Woodward, former religious editor for *Newsweek*:

> "One often hears among educated Catholics the phrase 'the institutional Church' used as a term of derision. How very

American and sociological, how naive to suppose that anything of value can survive without institutions. The early Christians would never have begotten a second-generation Church if the charismatic first generation did not develop institutions, chains of command, and eventually a hierarchy. Of course, the Church is more than the sum of its institutions. But no society can survive without institutions, which are not just buildings or chains of command, but also patterns of behavior. It is only through institutions that traditions are passed on, the young are brought up, the undisciplined disciplined, and society sustained including the society we call the Church."

"I have done my share of institutional criticism. There isn't a religious group, I suppose, that I haven't offended. But what offends me is the romantic notion that all the ills of the Church reside with the institution so that if only we could reform it, we ourselves would be better Christians. The truth quite often is the other way around."[17]

Ronald Rolheiser, a respected, bestselling author and spiritual director:

"…a century ago, a prominent Protestant theologian, Frederick Schleiermacher, pointed out that, separated from historical religion, the individual's quest for God, however sincere that search, produces the unconfronted life. Without church, we have more private fantasy than real faith. He submits that real conversion demands that eventually its recipient be involved in both the muck and the grace of actual church life." Yes, unanchored faith soon becomes "it's all about me."[18]

Let me close with one such fellow pilgrim who has given me comfort along the way. His name is Frank Sheed, husband, father, public speaker, defender of the faith, writer, publisher, and one privy to the faith and foibles of the Catholic Church. He wrote:

"We are not baptized into the hierarchy, do not receive the cardinals sacramentally, will not spend an eternity in the beatific vision of the pope. St. John Fisher could say in a public sermon,

'If the pope will not reform the curia, God will.' A couple of years later he laid his head on Henry VIII's block for papal supremacy, followed to the same block by Thomas More, who had spent his youth under the Borgia pope, Alexander VI, lived his early adulthood under the Medici pope, Leo X, and died for papal supremacy under Clement VIII, as time-serving a pope as Rome ever had.

"Christ is the point. I, myself, admire the present pope but even if I criticized him as harshly as some do, even if his successor proved to be as bad as some of those who have gone before, even if I sometimes find the Church as I have to live with it, a pain in the neck, I should still say that nothing a pope could do or say would make me wish to leave the Church, although I might well wish that *he* would leave.

"Israel, through its best periods as through its worst, preserved the truth of God's oneness in a world swarming with gods, and a sense of God's majesty in a world sick with its own pride. So, with the Church. Under the worst administration we could still learn Christ's truth, receive his life in the sacraments, be in union with him to the limit of our willingness. In awareness of Christ, I can know the Church as his mystical body, and we must not make our judgment by the neck's sensitivity to pain."

By all means, let us laypeople and clergy alike get busy with reform, but let's reform organically where it works best, *within* the Church. So, continue to make Mass Matter. So what if your neck hurts a little?

Discussion Questions

1. There is real effort in some quarters to bridge the gap between clergy and laity without negating the charisms of each. Do you have any suggestions?
2. Pope Francis has been striving to give the official Church a human face by his compassion and care. What can you do to present the Church in a positive light?

Pastoral Suggestion

As a way of connecting with the youth, once a year we had the blessing of new drivers at Mass. The parents with the car keys stood at one side of the sanctuary and the young drivers stood on the other side. After praying that the Lord would give them "sharpness of eye, keenness of hearing, and alertness of mind for in a new way precious human life is being entrusted to their care," I turned to the new drivers and asked them to repeat after me: "Before my parents and my faith community, I pledge: never to drink and drive/never to let anyone who is drinking drive my car. /I pledge I will drive safely/ for I know that driving is both a privilege and a responsibility. / I intend to remember the first and honor the second; for all life is precious. /God keep me and my friends safe. Amen.

Then the parents crossed the sanctuary and handed over the car keys.

AN AFTERWORD

I WAS GOING TO make these remarks in the Introduction, but I saved them till now because they were too strong, too distracting, and even misleading. They would have prejudiced the rest of the book. Now that we're at the end, what was always "between the lines" and alluded to can be written of forthrightly. Bear with me as I make my case that what follows belongs in a book on going to church.

In August of 2018, a Pennsylvania grand jury issued a report detailing the sexual abuse of some 1,000 children and teens by some 300 priests in the Dioceses of Pennsylvania (minus the Dioceses of Philadelphia and Altoona-Johnstown) during the 60s and 70s. The victims were mostly boys. The lurid details and graphic descriptions of systematic depravity were so awful that I had to discontinue reading them. What stood out were not only the degradations of the crimes but the cover-ups by bishops who reassigned predators and locked away knowledge of the crimes in a hidden vault. Since the 1990's such revelations had come out, but this was the first fully-detailed account of what took place. The Church was indicted, Catholics were shamed, and the public was repulsed. Most of the clerical predators and bishops of those times are dead and the statute of limitations still remains although there are calls to cancel it. Emboldened by Pennsylvania governors, other states are prepared to go the same route and so the revelations will continue.

The moral cost is incalculable. The financial cost is estimated at some $4 billion dollars, money we paid, money rerouted from worthy causes. On the docket are clericalism, secrecy, and, most of all, the bishops who are totally discredited. There are calls for the resignation of our bishops, just as the bishops of Chile resigned after the revelations of abuse surfaced there. Some American bishops may take that path. It's better than being jailed.

In the midst of this moral collapse, there inevitably arises the imperative of reform that will have to include oversight by, and collaboration and consultation with, the laity: men and women who will have an official seat at the policy table. Clericalism will be dismantled, and absolute power will give way to mutual partnership—collaborators, co-laborers, to use the phrase from this book. That's why I stressed the need to be an intentional Catholic, and the need to make the liturgy as clean and focused as possible. All those criticisms and practical suggestions about attitudes, the liturgy, priests, former Catholics, young and old, were not just quirky, whimsical, or pedantic; they were meant to prepare you for your old/new role: being Church.

I can't quite remember the source—I think it was in the *National Catholic Reporter*, but I have the clipping that says everything that inspired this book and is hidden in its pages:

> "The next time you go to Mass and as you kneel in that silence that envelopes the church before the liturgy begins, utter a prayer for this battered and wounded body we call the Church. Pray for a renewal and inspiration from the Holy Spirit, and pray for a reform of our broken system. Then glance to your left and your right. Kneeling beside you are likely the strongest allies you have in rebuilding a Church so badly in need of reform."

That truth is why I tell people who are thinking of leaving the Church, "Don't. Don't leave. Lead."

Mass Matters.

FOOTNOTES AND CREDITS

1. The quotation by Eamon Duffy is found in the British publication, *The Tablet*, 2 December 2017, "Broken English" by Eamon Duffy.

2. *The Christian Parish*, William J. Bausch, Twenty Third Publications, 1980, p 1.

3. *The Church in the Midst of Creation*, Vincent Donovan, (SCM, 1989).

4. Some of the insights are from an article by T.M. Luhrmann, a professor of anthropology at Sanford and the author of "When God Talks Back: Understanding the American Evangelical Relationship with God" and from an article from *The Wall Street Journal*, (12/29/17) plus some excerpts from "Psychologists Shouldn't Ignore the Soul" by David H. Rosmarin, Orthodox Jew, psychiatrist, and assistant professor of psychiatry at Harvard University.

5. *The Wall Street Journal*, January 6 2018, "We Can Encourage Our Better Angels." The quotation is from Timothy O'Malley's book, *Bored Again Catholic*, Ave Maria Press, 2017. p 17-18.

6. The Merton quote is from Timothy O'Malley, *op.cit.* p. 63.

7. *The New York Times*. November 12, 2017.

8. Some of the thoughts are from Rachel Held Evan's book, *Searching for Sunday*, Nelson Books. 2015.

9. Douglas Copeland, *Life After God*, Pocket Books, 1994.

10. Dorothy Fortenberry, *LARB Quarterly Journal*; No.12. June 8, 2017.

11. The data here is from an article by Hosfman Ospino in *America*, November 13, 2017, "The Hispanic Heart of the Church." There is a fine, free, newsletter that keeps abreast of Catholic Latinos. To sign up for it, visit https://www.americamag-azine.org/convivir.

12. Concerning the routine abortions of Down Syndrome babies, it is worth noting that in the days of Louis Pasteur a rabies-afflicted baby would be placed between two mattresses and smothered to spare him the terrible suffering. Pasteur, a devout Catholic, would not accept this and he treated a boy with rabies and the rest is history. Had he failed he would have been sent to prison and died in disgrace. With this in mind, read *Life is a Blessing: a Biography of Jerome Lejuene*. Lejuene, who died in 1994, was famous for discovering what caused Down Syndrome. He was awarded a medal by President Kennedy. Lejuene was appalled at the automatic abortions upon detection rather than pursuing a cure. "It is always easier to kill than to cure," he lamented. See *Magnificat*, February, 2018.

Concerning the growing euthanizing of Down syndrome babies, we note that in 2017 twenty-three-year-old Mikayla Holmgren became the first woman with Down syndrome to compete in a Miss USA pageant. She said she wanted to show the world that people with Down syndrome have beauty that starts from the inside out. "There are countries in the world" she noted, "that would like to get rid of people like me." The father of a daughter with Down syndrome said, "I can't think of any greater crime than identifying a population for termination because they don't live up to our culture's standard of perfection."

13. Some information was gleaned from the article, "Ministry and Millennials," by Zac David, *America*, October 30, 2017. Let me add three other relevant items:

First, we cannot dismiss the burdens which the Baby Boomers bequeathed to their children. They are indeed the best educated ever, but are far worse off economically than their parents and grandparents. So many are living at home with their parents. The job training they must undergo is onerous. The homework they get is three times as much as past generations. They are drowning in student loans and are less emotionally stable. They carry much more anxiety than the young people of fifty years ago. A good book to read in this regard is Malcolm Harris' *Kids These Days*, Little Brown and Company.

Secondly, we already noted in Chapter 13 how the young Hispanics, like young Americans in general, are dropping out of organized religion. Here, let me add that

Muslims are experiencing the same phenomenon. The number of American Muslims has increased by fifty percent in the past decade and, according to the Pew Research Center, twenty-three percent of Americans raised as Muslims—mostly the young second generation immigrants—no longer identify with their faith. We observe that, in most of their homelands, that might cost them their lives.

Finally, let me toss in this latest Pew Research Center survey that shows that most Americans believe in some kind of higher power, but not necessarily the God of the Old or New Testaments. In this regard, according to the survey, some ninety-two percent of Evangelical and African American Protestants believe in the God described in the Bible, but only nine percent of Catholics do. Interesting.

14. Sandra Marie Schneiders, "Religion versus Spirituality: A Contemporary Conundrum." Fall 2007, Spiritus, John Hopkins, Volume 3. No 2, Fall, 2007.

15. From his poem, "The Rock."

16. Andrew Greeley, *The Hesitant Pilgrim*.

17. *Commonweal*, September 9, 1994.

18. *The Holy Longing*, chapter 6.

ABOUT THE AUTHOR

William J. Bausch, a retired priest of the diocese of Trenton, is still active in parish ministry. He is the award-winning author of numerous books on parish ministry, the sacraments, Church history, storytelling, and homiletics. He has lectured and given workshops at such colleges and universities as Notre Dame; Sacred Heart in Fairfield, Connecticut; Boston College; Charles Carroll in Cleveland; and in most U.S. dioceses as well as abroad. His most recent book, *From No to Yes*, is a collection of 72 never-before-published homilies covering the liturgical cycles with an eye to contemporary issues. With his signature use of stories, Father Bausch engages us to enter into the ever ancient, ever new gospel of Jesus.